Popular Culture and World Politics: Theories, Methods, Pedagogies

EDITED BY
FEDERICA CASO AND CAITLIN HAMILTON

E-INTERNATIONAL
RELATIONS
PUBLISHING

E-International Relations
www.E-IR.info
Bristol, UK
2015

Series Editors: Stephen McGlinchey and Marianna Karakoulaki
Copy Editing: Michael Pang and Gill Gairdner
Production: Ran Xiao
Cover Image: Hagen411

E-International Relations is the world's leading open access website for students and scholars of international politics. The website was established in November 2007, and is run by a UK registered non-profit organisation staffed with an all-volunteer team. The website has over 200,000 unique visitors a month (2014 average) from a worldwide audience. We publish a daily range of articles, blogs, essays, reviews and interviews. Our venture into producing print copies of our publications, starting in 2015, has come as a result of demand from libraries, readers, and authors – but also to help us cover the significant costs of producing these publications.

As E-International Relations is committed to open access in the fullest sense, this book is also available as a free PDF download on the E-International Relations website on our publications page: http://www.e-ir.info/publications/

ISBN 978-1-910814-02-4
ISSN 2053-8626

Abstract

This edited collection brings together insights from some of the key thinkers working in the area of popular culture and world politics (PCWP). Offering a holistic approach to this field of research, it contributes to the establishment of PCWP as a sub-discipline of International Relations. The volume opens with some theoretical considerations that ground popular culture in world politics. It then looks at different sources of popular culture and world politics, along with some of the methods we can use to study them. It concludes with a discussion about some of the implications of bringing popular culture into the classroom. Canvassing issues such as geopolitics, political identities, the 'War on Terror' and political communication and drawing from sources such as film, videogames, art and music, this collection presents cutting-edge research and is an invaluable reader for anyone interested in popular culture and world politics.

Federica Caso is Associate Articles Editor of E-International Relations. She is currently finishing her second MA in Gender, Sexuality and Queer Theory, and is due to commence her PhD in July 2015 under the supervision of Professor Roland Bleiker at the University of Queensland, Australia. Her research investigates virtual embodiment and representations of gender in military video games with a view to understanding how they facilitate the circulation of a culture of militarised masculinity in the aftermath of 9/11.

Caitlin Hamilton is a PhD candidate at UNSW Australia. Her dissertation looks at how visual popular cultural media – including internet memes, street art, and graphic novels – function as political artefacts. She is currently the Managing Editor of the Australian Journal of International Affairs. She has also occupied multiple roles at E-International Relations, including Commissioning Editor and Articles Editor, and is currently a member of the website's Editorial Board.

Contents

Introduction

FEDERICA CASO
UNIVERSITY OF QUEENSLAND
AND
CAITLIN HAMILTON
UNSW AUSTRALIA

This collection brings together world politics and popular culture to challenge the disciplinary boundaries of International Relations (IR). The study of popular culture in world politics is not a particularly new development; since the 1990s, a growing number of IR scholars have engaged aesthetic sources and popular culture artefacts to address issues relating to the discipline of IR. Yet, this type of research is often still not welcomed in the social sciences. This is regrettable, as the advantages of bringing popular culture and world politics together are multiple; to name just a few, taking popular culture sources as sites of world politics encourages us to consider the role of visual politics and emotions in shaping the socio-political world (Bleiker 2001, 2009; Moore & Shepherd 2010); it complicates the hierarchy of sources of world politics (Weldes 2006); and it invites us to challenge the idea that world politics take place only in the public sphere (Enloe 1989, Dittmer & Gray 2010). In doing so, the bringing together of world politics and popular culture reanimates debates in IR and creates new spaces for critical reflection.

Moreover, the interest in popular culture has contributed to International Relations moving away from stagnant macro-political analyses focused on systemic relations between states to find new referents and highlight new dynamics of power. Displacing the assumption that IR theory is just about the production of knowledge on inter-state relations (Wight 1960), a focus on popular culture is a response to the call by some IR scholars to shift attention from the state to the individual. For example, while a video game might not resemble the sources that we are more used to studying, such as presidential statements, policy briefs, and treaties, it is still a site of micro-politics where political subjectivities, geopolitical and security imaginations, identities, and imagined communities are (re)produced at the level of the everyday (Power 2007; Robinson 2012; Salter 2011; Sisler 2008; Stahl 2006).

A focus on the complex relations between world politics and popular culture answers the call by many IR scholars to pay attention to micro-politics as well as macro-politics, the private alongside the public, the personal together with the political, and the dismantling of the dualistic oppositions that exist between these terms. Christine Sylvester (2001, pp. 824-5), for example, recognises that an inherent paradox in the discipline of IR is that, despite (according to one narrative, at least) it being born out of concerns with the devastating toll of war and violence against humans, IR has almost completely disengaged with issues concerning subjectivity, human bodies and the lived experiences of violence. Instead of this conception of world politics, she sees 'international relations [as] a place of people', with 'eyes peeking through cracks in the analysis and gazing out from everyday locations' (2013, p. 2). Steve Smith also acknowledges the flaws of an impersonal disciplinary IR, going so far as to accuse IR theory of being implicated in creating the world that led to the events of 11 September 2001. In particular, he contends that the focus of IR theory on the security of the state has come at the expense of the security of the individual (Smith 2004, pp. 504-5).

Having also identified these issues in the discipline, scholars such Jutta Weldes (1999) and Michael Shapiro (1999) have advocated the need for us to move beyond cultural and political elite settings towards mass and popular culture. This opens the epistemic space to study the complex relationships between popular culture and world politics (PCWP). In their seminal work on PCWP, Davies, Grayson and Philpott (2009) argue that world politics and popular culture ought not to be regarded as a series of intersecting points but as a continuum; the two spheres, they contend, are inseparable and inhabit the same space. Understanding world politics and popular culture as a continuum allows us to grasp the holistic nature of politics. This is in contrast to more conventional understandings of the relationship between these two arenas, forced into a Cartesian split with the former elevated to high politics and the latter to low data. As Weldes (2006, p. 185) points out, '[d] esignating some forms of data (or politics or culture) "low" is thus fundamentally an exercise of power, albeit one that tends to obscure its own functioning'. Neither popular culture nor politics are produced in social and political vacuums, and greater attention to the world politics-popular culture continuum can help to illuminate interstices of power that are overlooked by orthodox approaches to IR (Grayson, Davies & Philpott 2009).

The discipline of IR is well trained in dynamics of power and knowledge; entering the 'House of IR' implicitly means being involved in mechanisms of power relations and hierarchisation; IR does not hesitate to identify 'who's "in", who's "out", and who's precariously "on the border". It also stratifies who's "upstairs" and who's "downstairs"' (Angathangelou & Ling 2004, p. 23). While a number of IR scholars are working on popular culture in attempts to raise its profile, it remains the case that this area of study is kept on the doorstep, an uninvited and unwelcome guest, and there are a number of challenges to further developing this research agenda.

While established (and especially tenured) IR scholars find a way to publish on the topic, newcomers and would-be PhD students applying for funding are more vulnerable to the processes of marginalisation and even exclusion that result from working on the periphery of the discipline. It is not unusual to hear younger members of the profession cautioned away from studying popular culture; it is deemed acceptable as a side project, but to base your primary research on popular culture is still met with a great deal of resistance, particularly from older members of the discipline. We hope that this collection helps to counter this by contributing to the establishment of a legitimate sub-discipline of IR that deals with the intersection of world politics and popular culture.

While we were preparing this collection, two events received a great deal of global attention: the international response to the release of *The Interview* in December 2014 and, in early January 2015, the violent attacks in Paris – primarily on the offices of the satirical publication *Charlie Hebdo*. These events, along with the extensive media coverage that accompanied them, brought into stark relief the immense impact that popular culture artefacts can have on the international political landscape. These events, both of which transfixed the world's media, also made more apparent the role of popular culture as 'an interlocutor in world politics' (Saunders 2014). What these two cases show, as do the articles contained in this collection, is that it is simply no longer tenable to maintain that popular culture has nothing to do with world politics. The two are intimately and inextricably bound together. What is produced, consumed and 'prosumed' (Toffler 1980) in the cultural domain deserves far more attention than some IR scholars would care to admit.

This Edited Collection

With all of the above in mind, we have sought contributions from researchers who are working at the cutting edge of this research agenda. We have specifically invited some of the most prominent authors in the PCWP space to write for this collection, alongside PhD students and early-career scholars. We encouraged the authors of the articles contained in this volume to share ideas that were theoretically or methodologically orientated. The novelty value of popular culture sources can sometimes belie the rigorous scholarship and original research that underpins the field of PCWP, and we hope that this edited collection begins to address some of the scepticism with which this sort of research has been previously received. We also hope that the ideas that follow inspire and encourage more researchers to explore the many possibilities offered by this research agenda.

The collection opens with a set of articles that offer theoretical insights into the relationship between world politics and popular culture. In the first article, Jutta Weldes and Christina Rowley set a research agenda by offering six types of (interrelated) relations between world politics and popular culture, and explaining why they matter for the discipline of IR. These range from how states employ popular culture, including by rallying support through propaganda as well as by accruing soft power through cultural practices and events, to the global political economic implications of the production and consumption of popular culture. They consider the intertextuality of world politics and popular culture, as well as how popular culture is consumed differently according to geographical location.

The second article in our collection, by Constance Duncombe and Roland Bleiker, considers the ways in which popular culture is influential in shaping political identities and the narratives that sustain them. In particular, they argue that popular culture matters to world politics because of its visuality and that the emotions it conveys reinforce, shape and challenge prevailing identities in world politics. With a focus on US national identity, Duncombe and Bleiker discuss the ways in which political identities can be entrenched by popular culture, but also how they can be complicated and destabilised, and, beyond that, actively resisted and challenged. Images and emotions are both integral to all of these processes and, as a result, the authors argue, deserve greater scholarly attention.

The third article in this opening section comes from Jason Dittmer, who offers an insight into his experiences of studying PCWP, and shows how IR and political geography discipline (in a Foucauldian sense) the object of study. He argues that in order to understand the value of integrating popular culture and world politics, we need to reconceptualise popular culture as a *doing* rather than a *thing*; that is, not as a stand-alone cultural production but as the interaction between people, politics and cultural artefacts. He cautions against focusing on a single type of popular culture, instead urging us to look for connections, circulations and interactions – much as this collection seeks to do more broadly – because world politics and popular culture work in assemblage with each other. He also rightly points out that scholars interested in PCWP should focus more on the human body.

In Chapter 4, Klaus Dodds introduces the popular geopolitics of the war on terror. He identifies three different ways in which we can consider popular geopolitics, and particularly, its production and consumption. First, we can consider the politics of representation, paying attention to how places, ideas and communities are presented and signified within the popular culture artefact. A second way of analysing pop culture sources is to consider their affective qualities; in other words, how aspects such as lighting, costumes, locations and demeanours might impact viewers in a visceral sense. A third way of 'reading' popular culture in the context of critical popular geopolitics is to consider how intertextuality influences the various ways in which we can and do 'read' the world.

Linda Åhäll's contribution on 'The Hidden Politics of Militarization and Pop Culture as Political Communication' follows. In the first half of her article, Åhäll interrogates the concepts of militarism and militarisation using a feminist popular culture approach. She argues that the two terms are often erroneously used interchangeably, and suggests that the former is a belief and the second a process of normalisation. In the second half, she turns her attention to an advertisement for a fighter jet, offering a detailed and insightful reading of the ways in which the video perpetuates the normalisation of war and conflict, and how it functions as a form of political communication.

The second section of this collection addresses questions of methods and methodology. It opens with two powerful examples of how popular culture may disrupt our familiar ways of thinking about world politics, thus making it not only a tool for critique of the already existing but also a resource for thinking politics differently. In Chapter 6, Nick Kiersey and Iver Neumann direct our attention to the importance of genre when analysing world politics and popular culture. They focus on how science fiction as a genre might disrupt political expectations. Similarly, Chapter 7 by Michael Shapiro contends that the cinematic art is political because of the unique way that it challenges reality. Using *Hiroshima mon amour* (1959) as an example, Shapiro argues that cinematic forms and narrations can re-enact and reinterpret international political events in ways that challenge the official narrative.

Chapters 8 and 9 both focus on videogames and methods. Methods is a particularly challenging aspect of the study of videogames because, as Nick Robinson points out in Chapter 8, they are multi-sensorial media. He argues that not only must researchers grapple with the gameplay of videogames, but they must also take into account things such as the game's narrative, aural and visual aspects. He then discusses some of the methodological issues that can arise when we take videogames as our object of study, before identifying overlaps between Shapiro's idea of the aesthetic subject (2013) and videogames as a serious site of IR analysis. In the following chapter, written by Daniel Bos, we are introduced to the study of videogames in practice. Instead of analysing the videogames themselves, Bos directs his attention to the players of videogames. He suggests that taking a player-centred approach to these popular culture artefacts offers the possibility of new accounts of what it means to play war.

Chapters 10 and 11 introduce two more sources of popular culture that have received very little scholarly attention. In Chapter 10 we see Saara Särmä introduce the reader to 'Collage: An Art-inspired Methodology for Studying Laughter in World Politics'. Särmä's chapter offers insight into the potential of art as method and as a form of knowledge-production about the international realm, particularly where it appears in digital form in cyberspace. She shares her work, along with a number of thought-provoking ideas about disciplinary boundaries and inspiration as to how we might consider doing IR differently. In Chapter 11, Matt Davies and M.I. Franklin ask 'What Does (the Study of) World Politics Sound Like?' In this chapter, Davies and Franklin revisit some of the ideas first introduced in the 2005 edited collection *Resounding International Relations: on Music, Culture and Politics* (Franklin [ed.] 2005), and explore in detail some of the conceptual and methodological issues raised by the idea of auditory world politics.

The third and final section of this collection looks at some of the pedagogical issues relating to the use of popular culture in the IR classroom. All authors in this section have employed popular culture in their teaching and have identified both advantages and disadvantages to the inclusion of such sources. The section opens with Robert Saunders' contribution, entitled 'Imperial Imaginaries: Employing Science Fiction to Talk about Geopolitics'. After a discussion of science fiction as a genre and its importance for geopolitics, Saunders explains how he uses science fiction in the classroom and why it matters. Noteworthy is the fact that, contrary to Kiersey and Neuman in this collection, who take science fiction to be a genre of contestation, Saunders explores how it is instead implicated in imperial power and therefore how it can help the student to grasp the concept of imperialism. In Chapter 13, Kyle Grayson explores some of the challenges of incorporating popular culture sources into pedagogical practice and offers some valuable questions and cautions for educators who may be considering how best to use pop culture in their teaching. Finally, William Clapton provides the reader with an insight into his experience of drawing from popular culture in the classroom and in setting assessments in

Chapter 14. He discusses not only the ways in which he has found popular culture useful in his teaching but also – through his discussion of the feedback that he has received from students – how these sources are received in the classroom.

We offer our immense gratitude to the above authors for their wonderful contributions to this collection. All the ideas that we have had the privilege of engaging with have broadened and deepened our understanding of the multiple intersections and interweavings of popular culture and world politics and extended our appreciation of the complexity of this burgeoning sub-field of IR. We hope that the reader gets the same value and enjoyment out of the collection.

References

Agathangelou, A. M., & Ling, L. H. M. (2004) 'The House of IR: From Family Power Politics to the Poisies of Worldism', *International Studies Review*, 6(4): 21-49.

Bleiker, R. (2001) 'The Aesthetic Turn in International Political Theory', *Millennium – Journal of International Studies*, 30(3): 509-533.

Bleiker, R. (2009) *Aesthetics and World Politics*, Basingstoke: Palgrave Macmillan.

Grayson, K., Davies, M. and Philpott, S. (2009) 'Pop Goes IR? Researching the Popular Culture-World Politics Continuum', *Politics*, 29(3): 155-163.

Dittmer, J. & Gray, N. (2010) 'Popular Geopolitics 2.0: Towards New Methodologies of the Everyday', *Geography Compass*, 4(11): 1664-1677.

Enloe, C. (1989) *Bananas, Beaches, and Bases: Making Feminist Sense of International Relations*, Berkeley: University of California Press.

Franklin, M. (ed.) (2005) *Resounding International Relations: On Music, Culture, and Politics*, London: Palgrave Macmillan.

Moore, C. & Shepherd, L.J. (2010) 'Aesthetics and International Relations: Towards a Global Politics', *Global Society*, 24(3): 299-309.

Power, M. (2007) 'Digitized Virtuosity: Video War Games and Post-9/11 Cyber-Deterrence', *Security Dialogue*, 38(2): 271-288.

Robinson, N. (2012) 'Videogames, Persuasion and the War on Terror: Escaping or Embedding the Military-Entertainment Complex?', *Political Studies*, 60(3): 504-522.

Salter, M.B. (2011) 'The Geographical Imaginations of Video Games: Diplomacy, Civilization, America's Army and Grand Theft Auto IV', *Geopolitics*, 16(2): 359-388.

Saunders, R.A. (2014) 'The Interview and the Popular Culture-World Politics Continuum', *E-International Relations*, <http://www.e-ir.info/2014/12/23/situating-the-interview-within-the-popular-culture-world-politics-continuum/>.

Shapiro, M.J. (1999) *Cinematic Political Thought: Narrating Race, Nation and Gender*, Edinburgh: Edinburgh University Press.

Shapiro, M.J. (2013) *Studies in Trans-Disciplinary Method: After the Aesthetic Turn*, London: Routledge.

Sisler, V. (2008) 'Digital Arabs: Representation in Video Games', *European Journal of Cultural Studies*, 11(2): 203-220.

Smith, S. (2004) 'Singing Our World into Existence: International Relations Theory and September 11', *International Studies Quarterly*, 48(3): 499-515.

Stahl, R. (2006) 'Have You Played the War on Terror?', *Critical Studies in Media Communication*, 23(2): 112-130.

Sylvester, C. (2001) 'Art, Abstraction, and International Relations', *Millennium: Journal of International Studies*, 30(3): 535-554.

Toffler, A. (1980) *The Third Way*, New York: Bantam Books.

Weldes, J. (1999) 'Going Cultural: Star Trek, State Action, and Popular Culture', *Millennium: Journal of International Studies*, 28(1): 117-134.

Weldes, J. (2006) 'High Politics and Low Data: Globalization Discourses and Popular Culture', in D. Yanow & P. Schwartz-Shea (eds), *Interpretation and Method Empirical Research Methods and the Interpretive Turn*, London, New York: M.E. Sharper.

Wight, M. (1960) 'Why Is There No International Theory?', *International Relations*, 2(1): 35-48.

Part One

POPULAR CULTURE AND WORLD POLITICS: IN THEORY AND IN PRACTICE

So, How *Does* Popular Culture Relate to World Politics?

JUTTA WELDES
AND
CHRISTINA ROWLEY
UNIVERSITY OF BRISTOL

Introduction

Fifteen years ago it was necessary to argue that IR as a discipline ignored popular culture (Weldes 1999, p. 117). Happily, this is no longer the case. Some corners of what might be called 'mainstream IR' (but only quite narrowly construed and mostly North American) still implicitly or explicitly insist that popular culture is not worthy of scholarly IR attention, perhaps because it is seen as 'low' politics, domestic politics, or not political at all. However, scholars from assorted perspectives and disciplines are eagerly and productively investigating myriad forms of popular culture in relation to every conceivable aspect of IR and world politics.[1] One might even argue that there now exists a sub-(inter-)discipline of Popular Culture and World Politics (PCWP).[2]

In teaching a unit entitled 'Popular Culture and World Politics' – which Jutta first taught in the US in the 1990s and Christina and Jutta have taught/teach at the University of Bristol – we have been genuinely flummoxed by one thing. Some students invariably complain, well into or even at the end of the unit, 'But I don't understand – how *does* popular culture relate to world politics?'[3] Asking this question, given that the entire unit is organised around addressing it head on, indicates a 'stuckness' in a narrow understanding of IR (as discipline) or international relations (as state practice) or world politics (as a wider, but still conventional, set of trans-border practices). At the same time, this question reflects a further assumption, sometimes surprisingly difficult to shift, that there is/ought to be a simple, perhaps even singular, way to grasp how one 'thing' – popular culture – 'relates' (preferably causally) to another 'thing' – world politics. In typical positivist fashion, students often expect to find that popular culture 'does' something 'to' world politics (or, less often, that world politics 'does' something 'to' popular culture).

But these assumptions misunderstand. Analytically, both 'popular culture' and 'world politics' are complex and contested concepts, so there can be no singular understanding of either. Empirically, the objects and practices to which the terms refer, and the 'relations' between and among them, are varied, complex and dynamic. In this paper we take a

---

[1] We use IR to refer to use scholarly practices and theories, and 'world politics' to mean local, regional, national and global practices. This distinction, while problematic, is useful for our argument.

[2] See also www.pcwpnet1.wordpress.com and the Routledge PCWP book series. The interdisciplinary and international character of PCWP can be seen in the PCWP conferences: PCWP1, University of Bristol, 2008 (convened by us); PCWP2, Newcastle University, 2009 (Matt Davies, Kyle Grayson, Simon Philpott); PCWP3, York University, Toronto, 2010 (David Mutimer); PCWP4, University of Lapland, 2011 (Julian Reid, Laura Junka-Aikio), PCWP5, Hobart and Smith Colleges, Geneva, NY, 2011 (Kevin Dunn); PCWP6, Stockholm University, 2013 (Michele Micheletti, Kristina Riegert); PCWP7, University of Ottawa, 2014 (Mark Salter, Sandra Yao, David Grondin).

[3] This question, and its implied desire for certainty and singularity, resonates with Marysia Zalewski's (1995) question, 'Well, what is the feminist perspective on Bosnia?'.

preliminary stab at categorising analytically the relations that obtain between 'popular culture' and 'world politics' – and at suggesting why they matter. We present six types of relations between PC and WP, viewing each, in turn, as multfaceted and not unrelated to the others.[4] We then use the 'diamond engagement ring' to underscore the interconnections among these various relations.

A caveat is in order here: we are emphatically *not* precluding arguments about other possible relationships between popular culture and world politics. We wish to open up analytical spaces, not close them down. We want to show that there are already at least these very diverse (ways of understanding the) ways in which these 'things' relate to one another.[5] To paraphrase Robert Cox (1981, p. 128), these PCWP relationships matter to different audiences for diverse and sometimes competing reasons. This article thus highlights diverse ways in which these relationships matter (to us) in order to highlight how they should matter to more people, especially scholars and practitioners of world politics, in which we include the general public (Rowley and Weldes 2012). In so doing, we deliberately raise more questions than we can possibly answer. In highlighting the sheer breadth of what can be explored, we view this article as, in part, contributing to a very broad, but not definitive, PCWP research agenda.[6]

State Uses of Popular Culture

Perhaps the most obvious PCWP 'relation', at least for realist-inspired approaches/ analysts, is that states actively use popular culture in many ways and for multiple purposes.[7] In both wartime and peacetime, popular culture plays a surprisingly (or not?) large role in foreign (and domestic) policies.

In times of war, states (sometimes notoriously) create, deploy, and exploit popular culture as/for propaganda (Robb 2004, Aulich 2011). For instance, posters and other media forms were famously deployed to define nations and their enemies in WWI (War Propaganda 2014, Welch n.d., Oliver n.d.); North Vietnamese posters similarly constituted the US enemy in the 'American War' (see 'Decades of Protest').[8] Films like *Casablanca* (1942),

---

[4] Each of these types of relationship also has interesting teaching applications (for scholarly sources with a pedagogical focus, see e.g. Beavers 2002, Ruane and James 2008, Davies 2013, Weber 2014) but these are sadly beyond the scope of this article.

[5] We draw heavily on US and UK examples not because they are more important but because we are most familiar with these.

[6] We welcome suggestions of other relationships that we have unwittingly omitted.

[7] Non-state actors of course also deploy popular culture in similarly instrumental ways. The role of social media in the 'Arab Spring' is a case in point and has received considerable scholarly attention (e.g. Aouragh and Alexander 2011, Shirky 2011).

[8] 'Decade of Protest: Political Posters from the United States, Cuba and Vietnam 1965-1975', The Sixties Project, http://www2.iath.virginia.edu/sixties/HTML_docs/Exhibits/Track16.html.

backed by the 'War Films' division of the US Department of War, sold US intervention in Europe to US publics, legitimating World War II and the attendant military expenditures and public sacrifices (Tunc 2007). *The Green Berets* (1968), starring John Wayne, was so overtly a propaganda film that the US Department of Defense had the usual credit thanking it for its assistance removed, for fear that it might undermine the film's propaganda value and draw unwanted attention to the department's involvement in Hollywood films (Robb 2004, pp. 277-284).

States also deploy popular culture in times of peace. To develop 'soft power', states engage in cultural diplomacy practices that actively deploy popular culture (UK House of Lords 2014, Rowley 2014). The British Council[9] seeks to build trust by enhancing cultural relations through international collaborations in, among other areas, fashion, film, music, theatre and dance. Post-9/11 American cultural exchange programmes also emphasise popular culture, notably sports (see the US Department of State's SportsUnited Facebook page)[10] and film, in trying to refurbish the US image in 'Muslim countries' (Mills 2014). Popular culture features centrally in the increasingly pervasive state practice of nation-branding (Anholt 2014). 'Brand Turkey',[11] for example, defines itself using the foodways metaphor of the 'coffeehouse' while also invoking shopping, the bazaar, cinema and folk dancing. 'Cool Britannia', the Blair government's cringe-worthy attempt to sell the UK internationally, drew explicitly on 1960s-style dress, on 'Britpop' and on 'Young British Artists' such as Damien Hirst and Tracey Emin. The current 'Britain is GREAT'[12] incarnation showcases 'the very best of what Britain has to offer', invoking pop cultural resources including shopping, tourism, pubs, and cinema.

Sports play a diverse and particularly important role in foreign policy and state action. What famously became known as 'ping pong diplomacy' (DeVoss 2002) signalled a breakthrough in Cold War US-China relations when, in April 1971, 'at the invitation of the Chinese government, a nine-person United States table tennis team ... visited China for a series of exhibition matches' (Campagna 2011). This visit ultimately led to Nixon's visit to China and the re-establishment of US-China diplomatic relations (Griffin 2014). More mundanely, hosting the Olympics has long been desired by states to enhance their international status and showcase economic and cultural accomplishments (Schaffer and Smith 2000). The 1995 Rugby World Cup, held in South Africa, was a 'two-level' political 'game'.[13] Internationally, it signalled South Africa's post-Apartheid reintegration into the international

---

[9]   British Council, <http://www.britishcouncil.org/>.

[10]   SportsUnited – US Department of State, Facebook, <https://www.facebook.com/pages/SportsUnited-US-Department-of-State/10150101343025475>.

[11]   Brand Turkey, <http://turkayfe.org/index.php/brandturkey>.

[12]   'Britain is GREAT', GOV.UK, <https://www.gov.uk/britainisgreat>.

[13]   Robert Putnam's (1988) concept neatly reveals both the permeation of popular cultural terms in IR – the use of the 'game' metaphor – and the hierarchisation at work in the domestic/international binary.

community; domestically, it attempted to create a 'Rainbow Nation' as a new multicultural national identity (Steenveld and Strelitz 1998).[14]

The Global Political Economy and/of Popular Culture

Most forms of popular culture are produced and consumed in industrial form, and these industries, their inputs (raw materials, labour, technology), practices (of production and consumption), and outputs (films, clothing, toys, etc.) transcend state boundaries. Whatever International Political Economy (IPE) scholars study – whether international trade, finance or intellectual property rights regimes (or the subversion of these, e.g. counterfeit consumer goods); MNCs and global divisions of labour; the relations of states and markets; or international economic advance/North-South relations – popular culture is always already enmeshed in both the IPE disciplinary landscape and the fabric of international political economic practices.[15]

US-China trade relations, for example, have a massive popular cultural component. The five largest categories of goods exported by China to the US include furniture and bedding, toys and sports equipment, and footwear (US Executive Office of the President 2014), while top US exports to China include the raw materials (e.g. metals and plastics) to make these. In 2005, the US Department of State warned prospective business investors via the US Embassy in Beijing that, '[o]n average, 20 percent of all consumer products in the Chinese market are counterfeit'. Among the items violating copyright and trademark regulations were 'auto parts, watches, sporting goods, shampoo, footwear, designer apparel, medicine and medical devices, leather goods, toys'. On a more positive note, the State Department has also lauded the recent US-Chinese film industry collaboration, notably the creation of Oriental DreamWorks – a joint venture of DreamWorks, Shanghai Media Group and two additional Chinese firms – as signalling the potential for further joint economic development in industries like television, theme parks and merchandising, leading to increased economic growth (Rivkin 2014).

Conversely, popular cultural industries and franchises are worthy of study in their own right as microcosms of IPE (e.g. the practices of the global tourism, fashion or music industries; competition among Hollywood, Bollywood and Nollywood; the globalisation of Harry Potter [Nexon and Neumann 2005]; the *Star Wars* franchise and director George Lucas' companies Lucasfilm and Industrial Light and Magic). The Disney Corporation, for

---

[14] Again, this example is more complex than it initially appears. This World Cup became the subject of a globally popular 2009 film, which itself invoked the Victorian-era poem: Invictus (Henley 1988).

[15] On an intertextual note, in 1986, The Economist invented the 'Big Mac Index' as a 'light-hearted guide' to misaligned exchange rates. It has since shifted from being a trivial pop culture reference to being 'a global standard, included in several economic textbooks and the subject of at least 20 academic studies' (D.H. and RL.W. 2014).

instance, is itself an important global economic actor: it is involved in global intellectual property rights, trademark and copyright issues and disputes (Levin 2003); it competes with other brands internationally (Stewart 2006); it engages in economic diplomacy; it has a global workforce; it sources products globally; its consumer base is global.

Narrowing the focus from interstate economic relations and global industries to a single popular cultural artefact such as Cynthia Enloe's 'globetrotting sneaker' (2004, pp. 43-56) allows us to get at multiple dynamic intersections of (gendered) economics, politics and popular culture, including:

- The gendered dynamics of global production (sewing sneakers is feminised, management and security are masculinised);
- The gendered processes of migration and urbanisation (young, unmarried women in South Korea relocate to cities, sending home remittances) and the changes in gender relations that ensue;
- The gendered militarisation of economic production (US military bases protect export processing zones, in turn contributing to prostitution as a major base-related industry);
- The intersection of economics and security politics: during the Cold War, the US supported authoritarian regimes that prevented unionisation, keeping wages low; once the authoritarian regime, e.g. South Korea, 'fell' to democratisation – thereby allowing organised labour to demand better working conditions and wage rises – the sneaker trotted to the next US-supported, authoritarian, low-wage state, from (e.g.) South Korea/Taiwan to Indonesia, to Thailand, to China.

Using the node of the sneaker, Enloe thus draws our attention to the complexly intertwined and dynamic political economy of popular culture: the fundamental, structural inequalities and the diverse forms of power that must be exercised to ensure that the global economic system runs 'smoothly' and to keep a ready supply of fashionable footwear available for Western consumers.

Global Flows are Cultural and Political

Relatedly, but distinctly, popular culture is also a central component of the contested flows, practices and processes of – depending on one's politics – homogenisation (whether understood as Americanisation, Westernisation or modernisation), hybridisation (Bhabha 1996), cultural imperialism (Tomlinson 1991) or globalisation. A first, and very basic, point concerns the *ubiquity* of these flows and the recognition that much of what flows *is* popular cultural (see our arguments in the previous section and consider, for example, the combined global outputs of Hollywood, Bollywood and Nollywood). For most people, these flows are experienced in and through popular culture. For example, Americanisation might be experienced through the pervasiveness of the US TV show *Dallas*, while modernisation might be experienced through the ubiquity of television in general.

A second dimension of these flows and their consequences is their supposed *uniformity*, which raises questions of homogenisation and hybridisation. The spread of English, facilitated by British colonialism and US imperialism, was shaped not only through official political documents and processes but also through popular cultural artefacts, such as the canon of English literature taught in missionary schools. Globally, ever-increasing numbers of people speak and/or understand English (learnt not only formally but also by listening to lyrics in American music, interpreting advertising slogans, chatting with tourists, etc.). Some people bemoan the apparently relentless spread of the English language and Anglo-American culture, spurring organisations such as the Académie française to protect national language and culture. At the same time, English colonialism led to the development of heterogeneous forms of Pidgin, Creole and other vernaculars (e.g. Ebonics)[16] around the world. These dynamics have local, national and global implications, for example in the ways that political and legal processes invariably privilege those who speak 'properly': vernaculars remain languages of the street, of the kitchen table, of music, rather than languages of commerce, finance or governance.

As these examples indicate, things – capital, technology, development, democracy, popular culture – are assumed to flow from the metropole to the periphery. Interrogating popular culture, however, complicates *directionality*, a third dimension, allowing us to highlight reverse cultural flows and 'multidirectional flows' (Otmazgin and Ben-Ari 2012, p. 3). Substantial portions of US 'New Age' culture, for example, are transplants from Hinduism, Buddhism and indigenous American traditions (Berger 2003, pp. 12-14) and 'traditional Asian medicines, health and fitness practices and approaches to mental health', such as yoga and acupuncture, have successfully been disseminated to the West (van Elteren 2011, p. 160). Relatedly, immigrants bring their foodways with them, ultimately leading to cultural hybrids like chicken tikka masala. Immigrant foodways are often the basis for entrepreneurial activities, such as restaurants and grocery stores – initially supporting the diaspora communities, but, over time, also being frequented by the broader population. The wider acceptance of the incoming foodways is then linked to the integration of the immigrants, and their cultural practices more broadly, into a more multicultural society (Hackett 2013).

---

[16] Rickford, J.R. (no date) 'What is Ebonics (African American English)?', Linguistic Society of America, <http://www.linguisticsociety.org/content/what-ebonics-african-american-english>.

A fourth dimension – the *temporality* of these flows – can also be problematised through the lens(es) of popular culture. Although we tend to think of 'globalising' processes as the hallmark of capitalist (late or post-) modernity, such movements and flows, including popular cultural ones, well predate this era. As Amitav Ghosh (1992) wonderfully illustrates, extensive transnational trade relations existed between India and Egypt more than a millennium ago. Trading routes for popular cultural items (e.g. foods – tea, spices and salt – or textiles such as silk) linked the Mediterranean, the Horn of Africa, Arabia, India and East Asia, demonstrating that diverse and spatially distant parts of the world have long been more complexly interconnected than contemporary narratives of globalisation imply (e.g. Artzy 2007, Liu 2001).

World Politics/Popular Culture: Representations, Texts and Intertexts

Another form of relations concerns popular cultural *representations* of world politics. What most US Americans 'know' about the Arab-Israeli conflict, for example, comes from what they see, hear, and read in the news media – and, crucially, also what is presented in supposedly fictional popular cultural texts. This matters because media and cultural representations have political effects. Herman and Chomsky (1988, pp. 37-86) demonstrated that Cold War-era US news media gave differing amounts of attention to, for example, 'worthy' and 'unworthy' victims. One Polish priest, murdered by the communist Polish police, garnered far more attention and outrage than did 100 'religious personnel murdered in Latin America by [right-wing] agents of US client states' (p. 38), with the result that audiences see the Polish state as more threatening than US Latin American allies, thereby legitimating anti-communism on the one hand and right-wing paramilitary violence on the other.

This conceptualisation of the relations between PC and WP hinges on a 'reflection' metaphor, in which popular culture (whether news media, film or TV) is interrogated on (and frequently judged by) the extent to which it mirrors the 'real world'. However, the relationship is much more complex than this correspondence theory of truth allows.[17] Popular culture not only reflects but also *constitutes* world politics. Popular cultural texts discursively construct the objects about which they speak (Foucault, 1972, p. 49). Jack Shaheen (2009) demonstrates the overwhelmingly negative characteristics attributed to 'Arabs' in Hollywood films since the silent era. Disney's *Aladdin* (1992) provides a notable example, both in the grossly stereotypical visual representations of the Arab characters – Aladdin and Jasmine, as the protagonists, are of course exceptions, looking strikingly white

---

[17]   By a correspondence theory of truth, we mean the popular and generally unspoken belief that language, broadly understood, unproblematically refers to an equally unproblematised and distinct 'real world'.

and Western in comparison – and, quite controversially, in the original opening lyrics,[18] which were later replaced after complaints from, among others, the Arab-American Anti-Discrimination Committee (James 2009):

> Oh I come from a land, from a faraway place
> Where the caravan camels roam
> Where they cut off your ear
> If they don't like your face
> It's barbaric, but hey, it's home.

Similarly, through a variety of mechanisms (the 'ticking time bomb', the certainty that the person being tortured knows something, the hero's suffering about the moral dilemma), the television series *24* constructs torture as legitimate – indeed, as legitimate state policy – for the US (Mayer 2007, Van Veeren 2009). Anthropologist Lila Abu-Lughod (2010, p. 27) has shown that women in rural Egypt understand and interpret the pan-Islamic notion of 'Muslim women's rights' in part through representations of gender violence in popular national television serials like *A Matter of Public Opinion* (*Qadiya ra'y 'amm*). While popular cultural constructions are not the only sites in which identities, practices, institutions and objectives are discursively constituted, they are some of the most important. Popular culture is especially significant because we are all immersed in these discourses in our daily lives; they constitute our everyday common sense.

Popular cultural representations, moreover, are constructed intertextually. That is, the meanings of any one text depend on their being read in relation to other texts. And world politics and popular culture are very often read in relation to one another.[19] For example:

- While children can watch and enjoy the film *Chicken Run* (2000) without any knowledge of World War Two films, other viewers may make more complicated sense of the narrative and visual representations if they have seen *The Great Escape* (1963), which, in turn, itself represents, and can be intertextually interpreted in terms of, the Second World War in diverse ways.
- Popular debates about the 1980s US Strategic Defense Initiative (SDI) were conducted in terms of *Star Wars* (the 1977 film), with the result that SDI itself became known as 'star wars' (Weldes 2003, p. 2, Watkins Lang 2007).
- Globalisation is constituted in the frontier masculinity of adverts in *The Economist* (Hooper 2001).

---

18 'Arabian Nights Lyrics', Metro Lyrics, <http://www.metrolyrics.com/arabian-nights-lyrics-aladdin.html>

19 Which precise texts are read intertextually is contingent upon the reader and their familiarity, or lack thereof, with other texts.

- *Star Trek* represents both the light and the dark sides of US foreign policy (Weldes 1999).
- Both 'war' and 'sport' are frequently made intelligible through what Shapiro (1989) has dubbed the 'sport/war intertext'.
- We have written about these and other intertextual relationships extensively elsewhere (Weldes 2001, Rowley 2010a).

It is important to note that this argument is not just about the construction, deployment and effects of stereotypes simplistically understood. Textual meanings are made through much more complex processes, which include the diverse ways in which visual and narrative elements of texts interact (Rowley 2010b).[20]

The Politics of Cultural Consumption and Cultural Practices

While constructions are latent within texts (that is, texts contain potential readings), discursive labour is required to realise these. A subject's identity positions (we deliberately stress the plurality) do not determine how a text will be read/consumed/interpreted, but create the spaces for diverse readings to be actively articulated. One viewer of *Rambo: First Blood Part II* (1985), for instance, may revel in the combat scenes and find support for their brand of US national patriotism and valorisation of the veteran; another may find the racial and gender dynamics of the film highly problematic and read into the film a critique of US popular culture and/or US foreign policy.

The politics of consumption extends beyond merely acknowledging that popular cultural artefacts are consumed in diverse ways. Consumption is inextricably linked to the production and re-production of meanings – the maintenance of some, the transformation of others (whether through subversion, overt challenge or gradual change). In some cases, these processes of production, challenge and transformation are overtly highlighted. For example, the satirical response[21] response to an Australia.com tourism commercial[22] reflects explicitly, and quite critically, on the status of immigrants and racial dynamics in Australian society. However, these processes of discursive re-production, maintenance and transformation are always already at work, whether we explicitly reflect on participating in them or not. When hip-hop 'travels' from the US to Sierra Leone (Lock 2005) or Indonesia (van Wichelen 2005), it does not 'stay' American. The music and those who produce and

---

[20] The analysis of visual, cultural, textual representations, although not conducted from identical theoretical more methodological standpoints, constitutes by far the largest body of PCWP literature within IR – too large to review adequately here.

[21] YouTube (2006) 'Where the bloody hell are you?' video spoof, uploaded 13 September 2006, <https://www.youtube.com/watch?v=411ueiat2sY>.

[22] YouTube (2006) 'Where the bloody hell are you?' video advertisement, uploaded 20 March 2006, <https://www.youtube.com/watch?v=rn0lwGk4u9o>.

consume it are entangled in complex and transformative processes of meaning- and identity-making.

This discussion of consumption has thus far focused on the consumption of texts. However, consumption as a practice highlights the more general importance of cultural practices. Grocery shopping – a ubiquitous popular cultural practice – is interconnected with all sorts of political discourses and choices, around fair trade, organic produce, luxury, food miles, nutrition, development, value for money and animal welfare (to name just a few). Understanding people's shopping habits – how they justify their shopping choices, in which discursive terms they comprehend their place in the world, the emotional connections they have to certain brands, objects, behaviours – all of these form part of the dizzying complexity of this PC-WP relationship.[23]

We began with the politics of state uses of popular culture; here we wish to make the point that all of us are immersed in PCWP relationships. Indeed, the involvement of all of us in these relationships has been a tacit theme of all the preceding sections: we are the publics who decode state propaganda (sometimes accepting, sometimes rejecting various elements); we buy Disney toys and visit Disney World; we create and patronise the restaurants on our high streets; we watch films, TV and YouTube.

The Many Facets of the Diamond[24]

The diamond engagement ring links popular culture and world politics in a surprising number of ways. In this final section, we deploy that ring – an ostensibly frivolous, and highly gendered, symbol of tradition and romance – as a springboard to highlight the intimate and complex interconnections between and among the six PCWP relationships outlined above.[25]

Engagement rings, even in the West, have not always featured diamonds. This 'tradition', and the association of diamonds with eternal love and romance, was invented in the advertising campaigns of the diamond cartel De Beers. In 1947, the famous tagline 'A Diamond Is Forever' (ranked top advertising slogan of the twentieth century by Ad Age in 1999) was created for De Beers. It became De Beers' official motto in 1948 and has since accompanied all De Beers engagement ring advertising. Through this slogan, and massive

---

[23]   We have not discussed the emotional dimensions of PCWP in any depth here, but this is an as yet particularly underexplored dynamic (see Crawford 2003, Bleiker and Duncombe 2015, and Dodds 2015 in this collection).

[24]   For a well-developed conceptualisation of 'facets' and research methodology, see Mason (2011).

[25]   We recognise that our construction of this example privileges world politics over popular culture by forcing the diamond ring to prove its relevance to the latter, thus reproducing the privileging of WP over PC that we challenge in this article.

advertising campaigns built upon it – notably involving radio, television and print media reports about royalty and other celebrities sporting diamond jewellery – De Beers created a popular cultural myth on the basis of which it successfully revitalised US diamond sales, which had been falling dramatically since the Great Depression (Sullivan 2013, Epstein 1982).[26] De Beers later effectively deployed this 'market driving' strategy, in which a company seeks 'to reshape, educate and lead the consumer, or more generally, the market' (Harris and Cai 2002, p. 173) – or, in other words, engages in economic propaganda – to transplant these Western-invented matrimonial representations and practices to Japan in the 1970s (Epstein 1982) and to China in the 1990s and beyond, where diamonds are perceived as white and thus unlucky (Harris and Cai 2002, p. 181). The diamond engagement ring, and its seemingly obvious popular cultural 'meaning', is the product of the global marketing practices of a major commercial cartel and an instance of cultural globalisation.

Because of the location of its raw material – the uncut diamond – this cartel, and the trade more generally, is implicated not only in global marketing but also in African politics and particularly in specific forms of African civil and international conflicts. The illicit diamond trade (sustained initially by Western and latterly by more global consumption) has been used to finance 'rebels' and thus to fuel war, while various African states also benefit (through taxation and other means) from the 'licit' diamond trade. States regulate the diamond trade in various ways, including through labour regulation, the regulation of mines' and miners' health and safety, and, most recently, the regulation of 'conflict diamonds' in/ from states such as Sierra Leone, DRC, Angola, Liberia and Côte d'Ivoire (Jakobi 2013; see also UNSCR 1385 [2001]). The Kimberley Process[27] Certification Scheme – a joint initiative of governments, industry and civil society – established in 2003, attempts to regulate uncut diamond production and trade. Buying your 'sweetheart' a diamond ring or your 'mistress' a tennis bracelet is thus an everyday consumptive practice with world political implications involving a wide range of international actors. Whether diamond consumers consciously reflect on it or not, they are complicit in a luxury trade (which contributes to the reproduction of global economic inequalities) and also, potentially, in the unethical undercurrents of 'blood diamonds' (see, e.g., the Human Trafficking Movie Project n.d.).

The concept of the 'blood diamond', too, is part of other aspects of popular culture, having been globally popularised by the eponymous film (2006) starring Leonardo DiCaprio (himself a world political as well as a film actor, with his producer/executive producer roles

---

[26]   During this early advertising campaign, Queen Elizabeth II – who makes another diamond-studded appearance below – visited several South African diamond mines and 'accepted a diamond from [Harry] Oppenheimer', Chairman of De Beers, thus adding another overtly world politics dimension (Epstein 1982).

[27]   Kimberley Process, (n.d.) 'The Kimberley Process (KP)', <http://www.kimberleyprocess.com>.

on such documentaries as *The 11th Hour* [2007] and *Virunga* [2014]). *Blood Diamond* and Kanye West's award-winning song 'Diamonds from Sierra Leone' (which samples Shirley Bassey's chorus from 'Diamonds are Forever' – see below) drew the problem of 'blood diamonds' to media and public attention, while simultaneously constructing this issue in specific ways. In particular, the film reproduces the colonialist representation of Africa as relentlessly chaotic, dangerous, backward, etc. In contrast, and while simultaneously encouraging licit diamond consumption, West deliberately draws attention to the complicity of US blood diamond consumers (himself included), linking their purchases with conflict in Africa. And he goes further, connecting the violence of the blood diamond trade with the drug-fuelled, violent 'bling' culture of parts of urban US. Interestingly, in a striking example of intertextuality, films such as *Blood Diamond* now provide the interpretive frame used by Western news media to discuss these issues (Sharma 2012).

Intertextuality similarly defines *Diamonds are Forever*, the 1971 film, part of the globally successful Cold War 007 franchise, in which British spy James Bond simultaneously combats South African diamond smuggling and an interconnected global nuclear threat. The film's title song, sung by Shirley Bassey, together with 'Diamonds are a Girl's Best Friend' (from *Gentlemen Prefer Blondes* [1953], famously performed by Marilyn Monroe and also included in *Moulin Rouge* [2001]), and Madonna's 'Material Girl', all construct – in complex ways – the diamond, and diamond jewellery, as integral to women's identities and relationships with men. On the one hand they represent the diamond ring as a quintessential symbol of (heterosexual) romantic love and eternal attachment. On the other, however, women gain financial security from their expensive jewellery and sometimes have a more reliable relationship with the trustworthy jewel(lery) (Capon 2013). In some contexts (and contra the 'eternal love' trope), the diamond engagement ring offered, or was thought to offer, a financial surety for women who had consented to sex before marriage with their fiancés and were subsequently jilted (O'Brien 2012).

Finally, the diamond (and jewellery more generally) regularly appears in state diplomacy, perhaps most notably in the UK. The famous Indian Koh-i-Noor diamond, presented to Queen Victoria in 1850 (as a spoil of war), was set into the British Crown Jewels in 1937 (Nelson 2010, Tweedie 2010, see also The British Monarchy website.)[28] This diamond (and others in the Crown's possession) remains contentious symbols of British colonialism and exploitation. India recently demanded, again, that it be returned; UK Prime Minister David Cameron again refused (Groves 2010, BBC 2010). Queen Elizabeth II is regularly gifted with diamonds and other precious stones and jewellery, some of which, when the Queen functions as 'the personification and symbol of Britain to the outside world' (Jay 1992, p. 81), are deliberately redeployed as/in public diplomacy. When the Queen visits New Zealand, for example, she wears the diamond fern brooch given to her by 'the women of

---

[28]   The official website of the British Monarchy, 'The Crown Jewels', <http://www.royal.gov.uk/the%20 royal%20collection%20and%20other%20collections/thecrownjewels/overview.aspx>.

Auckland' on her first tour of New Zealand in 1953 (Tapaleao 2014); it was similarly worn, more recently, by the Duchess of Cambridge (English 2014). While these particular diamonds do not represent romance, they do represent state identities and the undying allegiance of the New Zealand 'people' to the British Commonwealth and monarchy (classic international relations to which popular culture ostensibly does not relate).

The diamond engagement ring – which looks at first glance to be a minor popular culture artefact 'about' romance – thus turns out to be intimately and complexly intertwined with a multitude of (themselves interconnected) world political actors, processes, practices, meanings and flows.

Some Conclusions

In examining diverse relations between 'popular culture' and 'world politics', we have also problematised the 'international' and the 'relations' in IR. We have opened the black box of 'popular culture' to examine the actors, institutions, processes, texts, sites and practices connected with it. As a result, 'world politics' looks broader and more complex than it did, shifting from a narrow focus on supra-/trans-/international state relations and practices, to trans-border practices by powerful non-state actors, to increasingly seeing the sub-national/regional and hyper-local – the everyday, in fact – as globally and politically implicated. However, as we have already noted, problematising world politics by highlighting popular culture, while challenging world politics, also continues to privilege it, to reinforce its status. We hope for the day when we no longer need to explain or justify how and why popular culture is relevant to world politics and can just get on with studying it.

While we have attempted not to judge the relative value of the six relationships that we have outlined, it should be clear that they are not all based on the same underlying assumptions about the world and how we can 'know' or study it. The massive analytical cost that comes with simplifying (reducing) the complexity of the world, of people, of processes and practices, has all too frequently been understated, ignored or denied in the pursuit of abstract models, laws and patterns. We have tried to demonstrate that the sheer volume and inherent messiness of the everyday – people's everyday lives, practices, meanings and identities, within which popular culture is embedded and of which it is constitutive – is intrinsically and significantly related to questions of world politics. As Enloe (1996) has famously argued, despite its focus on power, IR radically underestimates the amounts and types of power needed for 'world politics' to function as 'it' does. Examining the everyday phenomena that 'are' popular culture helps us to grasp the centrality of the many 'margins, silences and bottom rungs' of world politics.

References

The 11th Hour (2007) film, L. Conners (Petersen) and N. Conners (dirs.) <http://www.imdb.com/title/tt0492931/> [accessed 26 November 2014].

Abu-Lughod, L. (2010) 'The active social life of "Muslim women's rights": A plea for ethnography, not polemic, with cases from Egypt and Palestine', *Journal of Middle East Women's Studies*, 6(1): 1-45.

Ad Age (1999) 'Ad Age Advertising Century: Top 10 slogans', 29 March, <http://adage.com/article/special-report-the-advertising-century/ad-age-advertising-century-top-10-slogans/140156/> [accessed 27 November 2014].

Aladdin (1992) film, R. Clements and J. Musker (dirs), <http://www.imdb.com/title/tt0103639/> [accessed 27 November 2014].

Anholt, S. (2014), 'Written evidence', in UK House of Lords, Select Committee on Soft Power and the UK's Influence, 'Persuasion and power in the modern world', Report of Session 2013-14, 28 March, HL Paper 150, pp. 65-66, <http://www.parliament.uk/documents/lords-committees/soft-power-uk-influence/soft-power-ev-vol2-h-z.pdf> [accessed 24 November 2014].

Aouragh, M. and A. Alexander (2011) 'The Egyptian experience: Sense and nonsense of the Internet Revolution', *International Journal of Communcations*, 5: 1344-1358.

Artzy, M. (2007) 'Incense, camels and collared rim jars: Desert trade routes and maritime outlets in the second millennium', *Oxford Journal of Archaeology*, 13(2): 121-147.

Aulich, J. (2011) *War Posters: Weapons and Mass Communication*, London: Thames & Hudson.

BBC (2010) 'Koh-i-Noor diamond "staying put" in UK says Cameron', BBC News online, 29 July 2010, <http://www.bbc.co.uk/news/uk-politics-10802469> [accessed 28 November 2014].

Beavers, S. L. (2002) 'The *West Wing* as a pedagogical tool', *PS: Political Science & Politics*, 35(2): 213-216.

Berger, P. L. (2003) 'Introduction', in P. L. Berger and S. P. Huntington (eds), *Many Globalizations: Cultural Diversity in the Contemporary World*, Oxford: Oxford University Press, 1-16.

Bhabha, H. (1996) 'Culture's in-between', in S. Hall and P. du Gay (eds), *Questions of Cultural Identity*, London: Sage, 53-60.

Bleiker, R. and C. Duncombe (2015) 'Popular culture and political identity', in Caso, F. and Hamilton, C. (eds), *Popular Culture and World Politics: Theories, Methods, and Pedagogies*, E-IR, <http://www.e-ir.info/>.

Blood Diamond (2006) film, E. Zwick (dir.), <http://www.imdb.com/title/tt0450259/> [accessed 26 November 2014].

Campagna, J. (2011) 'Connie Sweeris, ping-pong diplomat', *Smithsonian Magazine*, 20 March, <http://www.smithsonianmag.com/arts-culture/connie-sweeris-ping-pong-diplomat-1094661/> [accessed 24 November 2014].

Capon, F. (2013) 'Are diamonds still a girl's best friend in 2013?', *The Telegraph*, 28 March, <http://www.telegraph.co.uk/women/womens-life/9959072/Are-diamonds-still-a-girls-best-friend-in-2013.html> [accessed 26 November 2014].

Casablanca (1942) film, M. Curtiz (dir.), <http://www.imdb.com/title/tt0034583/> [accessed 24 November 2014].

Chicken Run (2000) film, P. Lord and N. Park (dirs), <http://www.imdb.com/title/tt0120630/> [accessed 25 November 2014].

Cox, R. (1981) 'Social forces, states and world orders: Beyond international relations theory', *Millennium*, 10(2): 126-155.

Crawford, N. (2003) 'Feminist futures: Science fiction, utopia, and the art of possibilities in world politics', in J. Weldes (ed.), *To Seek out New Worlds: Science Fiction and World Politics*, New York: Palgrave Macmillan, 195-220.

Davies, M. (2013) 'Teaching IR with popular culture', *E-IR*, 26 June, <http://www.e-ir.info/2013/06/26/teaching-ir-with-popular-culture/> [accessed 25 November 2014].

DeVoss, D. A. (2002) 'Ping-pong diplomacy', *Smithsonian Magazine*, April, <http://www.smithsonianmag.com/history/ping-pong-diplomacy-60307544/> [accessed 25 November 2014].

D.H. & RL.W. (2014) 'The Big Mac Index', *The Economist*, 24 July, <http://www.economist.com/content/big-mac-indexv> [accessed 24 November 2014].

Diamonds Are Forever (1971) film, G. Hamilton (dir.), <http://www.imdb.com/title/tt0066995/> [accessed 26 November 2014].

Dodds, K. (2015), 'Popular geopolitics and the War on Terror', in F. Caso and C. Hamilton (eds), *Popular Culture and World Politics: Theories, Methods, and Pedagogies*, E-IR, <http://www.e-ir.info/>.

The Economist (2014) website, <http://www.economist.com/> [accessed 24 November 2014].

van Elteren, M. (2011) 'Cultural globalization and transnational flows of things American', in P. Pachura (ed.), *The Systemic Dimension of Globalization*, <http://www.intechopen.com/books/the-systemic-dimension-of-globalization/cultural-globalization-andtransnational-flows-of-things-american> [accessed 25 November].

English, R. (2014) 'Gorgeous George: Regal in red Kate wears Queen's New Zealand brooch as she arrives in Wellington… but it's her baby prince who steals the show', *Mail Online*, 6 April, <http://www.dailymail.co.uk/news/article-2598337/Duke-Duchess-Cambridge-begin-New-Zealand-Australia-tour-Prince-George.html> [accessed 1 December 2014].

Enloe, C. (1996) 'Margins, silences and bottom rungs: How to overcome the underestimation of power in the study of international relations', in S. Smith, K. Booth and M. Zalewski (eds), *International Theory: Positivism and Beyond*, Cambridge: Cambridge University Press, 186-202.

Enloe, C. (2004) *The Curious Feminist: Searching for Women in a New Age of Empire*, Berkeley, CA: University of California Press.

Epstein, E. J. (1982) 'Have you ever tried to sell a diamond?', *The Atlantic Online*, February, <http://www.theatlantic.com/past/issues/82feb/8202diamond1.htm> [accessed 27 November 2014].

Foucault, M. (1972) *The Archaeology of Knowledge and the Discourse on Language*, A. M. Sheridan Smith (trans.), New York: Pantheon Books.

Gentlemen Prefer Blondes (1953) film, H. Hawkes (dir.), <http://www.imdb.com/title/tt0045810/> [accessed 26 November 2014].

Ghosh, A. (1992) *In an Antique Land*, London: Granta.

The Great Escape (1963) film, J. Sturges (dir.) <http://www.imdb.com/title/tt0057115/> [accessed 25 November].

The Green Berets (1968) film, R. Kellogg, J. Wayne, M. LeRoy (dirs), <http://www.imdb.com/title/tt0063035/> [accessed 25 November 2014].

Griffin, N. (2014) *Ping-Pong Diplomacy: The Secret History behind the Game that Changed the World*, New York: Scribner.

Groves, J. (2010) 'David Cameron ambushed on Indian TV over 105-carat Koh-i-noor diamond as country demands its return', *Mail Online*, 29 July, <http://www.dailymail.co.uk/news/article-1298541/David-Cameron-ambushed-Indian-TV-105-carat-Koh-noor-diamond.html> [accessed 26 November 2014].

Hackett, S. E. (2013) 'From rags to restaurants: Self-determination, entrepreneurship and integration amongst Muslim immigrants in Newcastle upon Tyne in comparative perspective, 1960s-1990s', *Twentieth Century British History*, 25(1):132-154, [accessed 28 November 2014].

Harris, L. C. and K. Y. Cai (2002) 'Exploring market driving: A case study of De Beers in China', *Journal of Market-Focused Management*, 5(3): pp. 171-196, [accessed 27 November 2014].

Henley, W. E. (1888) 'Invictus', poem, <http://www.poetryfoundation.org/poem/182194> [accessed 24 November 2014].

Herman, E. S. and N. Chomsky (1988) *Manufacturing Consent: The Political Economy of the Mass Media*, New York: Pantheon.

Hooper, C. (2001) *Manly States: Masculinities, International Relations and Gender Politics,* New York: Columbia University Press.

Human Trafficking Movie Project (n.d.) website, <http://humantraffickingmovie.com/stopping-blood-diamonds.html> [accessed 26 November 2014].

Invictus (2009) film, C. Eastwood (dir.), <http://www.imdb.com/title/tt1057500/> [accessed 24 November 2014].

Jakobi, A. P. (2013) 'Governing war economies: Conflict diamonds and the Kimberley Process', in K. D. Wolf and A. P. Jakobi (eds), *The Transnational Governance of Violence and Crime: Non-State Actors in Security*, Basingstoke and New York: Palgrave Macmillan, 84-105.

James, R. (2009) 'Top 10 Disney controversies', *Time*, 9 December, <http://entertainment.time.com/2009/12/09/top-10-disney-controversies/slide/aladdin/> [accessed 9 January 2015].

Jay, A. (1992) *Elizabeth R. The Role of the Monarchy Today*, London: BBC Books.

Levin, B. (2003) *The Pirates and the Mouse: Disney's War against the Counter-Culture*, Seattle, WA: Fantagraphics Books.

Liu, X. (2001) 'The silk road: Overland trade and cultural interactions in Eurasia', in M. Adas (ed.), *Agricultural and Pastoral Societies in Ancient and Classical History*, Philadelphia: Temple University Press, 151-179.

Lock, K. (2005) 'Who is listening? Hip-hop in Sierra Leone, Liberia and Senegal', in M. I. Franklin (ed.), *Resounding International Relations: On Culture, Music, and Politics*, New York: Palgrave Macmillan, 141-160.

Mason, J. (2011) 'Facet methodology: The case for an inventive research orientation', *Methodological Innovations Online*, 6(3): 75-92, <http://www.methodologicalinnovations.org.uk/wp-content/uploads/2013/11/MIO63Paper31.pdf> [accessed 26 November 2014].

Mayer, J. (2007) 'Whatever it takes: The politics of the man behind "24"', *The New Yorker*, 19 February, <http://www.newyorker.com/magazine/2007/02/19/whatever-it-takes> [accessed 25 November 2014].

Mills, L. (2014) *Post-9/11 American Cultural Diplomacy: The Impossibility of Cosmopolitanism*, unpublished PhD thesis, Queens University Belfast.

Moulin Rouge (2001) film, B. Luhrmann (dir.), <http://www.imdb.com/title/tt0203009/> [accessed 26 November 2014].

Nelson, D. (2010) 'India demands return of Koh i Noor diamond', *The Telegraph*, 2 June, <http://www.telegraph.co.uk/news/worldnews/asia/india/7798130/India-demands-return-of-Koh-i-Noor-diamond.html> [accessed 26 November 2014].

Nexon, D. and I. B. Neumann (2006) *Harry Potter and International Relations*, Lanham, MD: Rowman & Littlefield.

O'Brien, M. (2012) 'The strange (and formerly sexist) economics of engagement rings', *The Atlantic*, 5 April, <http://www.theatlantic.com/business/archive/2012/04/the-strange-and-formerly-sexist-economics-of-engagement-rings/255434/> [accessed 25 November 2014].

Oliver, N. (n.d.) 'Was World War One propaganda the birth of spin?', BBC News, <http://www.bbc.co.uk/guides/zq8c7ty> [accessed 25 November 2014].

Otmazgin, N. and B. Eyal (eds) (2012) *Popular Culture and the State in East and Southeast Asia*, Abingdon and New York: Routledge.

Putnam, R. D. (1988) 'Diplomacy and domestic politics: The logic of two-level games', *International Organization*, 42(3): 427-460 [accessed 28 November 2014].

Rambo: First Blood Part II (1985) film, G. P. Cosmatos (dir.) <http://www.imdb.com/title/tt0089880/b> [accessed 26 November 20014].

Rivkin, C. H. (2014) 'Building a dynamic US-China film relationship', *The Economic Observer*, Beijing, 5 September, reposted by the US Department of State, <http://www.state.gov/e/eb/rls/rm/2014/231307.htm> [accessed 27 November 2014].

Robb, D. (2004) *Operation Hollywood: how the Pentagon Shapes and Censors the Movies*, New York: Prometheus Books.

Rowley, C. (2010a) *An Intertextual Analysis of Vietnam War Films and US Presidential Speeches*, unpublished PhD thesis, University of Bristol.

Rowley, C. (2010b) 'Popular culture and the politics of the visual', in L. J. Shepherd (ed.), *Gender Matters in Global Politics: A Feminist Introduction to International Relations*, London and New York: Routledge, 309-325.

Rowley, C. (2014) '*Written evidence*' in UK House of Lords, Select Committee on Soft Power and the UK's Influence, 'Persuasion and power in the modern world', Report of Session 2013-14, 28 March, HL Paper 150, pp. 801-806, <http://www.parliament.uk/documents/lords-committees/soft-power-uk-influence/soft-power-ev-vol2-h-z.pdf> [accessed 24 November 2014].

Rowley, C. and J. Weldes (2012) 'The evolution of international security studies and the everyday: Suggestions from the Buffyvere', *Security Dialogue*, 43(6): 513-530.

Ruane, A. E. and P. James (2008) 'The International Relations of Middle-Earth: Learning from *The Lord of the Rings*', *International Studies Perspectives*, 9(4): 377-394.

Schaffer, K. and S. Smith (eds) (2000) *The Olympics at the Millennium: Power, Politics, and the Games*, New Brunswick, NJ: Rutgers University Press.

Shaheen, J. (2009) *Reel Bad Arabs: How Hollywood Vilifies a People*, updated edition, Northampton, MA: Olive Branch Press.

Shapiro, M. (1989) 'Representing world politics: The sport/war intertext', in J. Der Derian and M. Shapiro (eds), *International/Intertextual Relations: Postmodern Readings of World Politics*, Lexington, Massachusetts: Lexington Books, 69-96.

Sharma, R. (2012) 'News on the rocks: Exploring the agenda-setting effects of Blood Diamond in print and broadcast news', *Media, War & Conflict* 5(3): 239-253.

Shirky, C. (2011) 'The political power of social media', *Foreign Affairs*, 90(1): 28-41.

Star Wars: Episode IV – A New Hope (1977) film, G. Lucas (dir.), <http://www.imdb.com/title/tt0076759/> [accessed 25 November 2014].

Steenveld, L. and L. Strelitz (1998) 'The 1995 Rugby World Cup and the politics of nation-building in South Africa', *Media, Culture & Society*, 20(4): 609-629.

Stewart, J. B. (2006) *Disney War*, New York: Simon and Schuster.

Sullivan, J. C. (2013) 'How diamonds became forever', *New York Times*, 3 May, <http://www.nytimes.com/2013/05/05/fashion/weddings/how-americans-learned-to-love-diamonds.html> [accessed 27 November 2014].

Tapaleao, V. (2014), 'Hunt on for origins of silver fern brooch', *The New Zealand Herald*, 10 April, <http://www.nzherald.co.nz/nz/news/article.cfm?c_id=1&objectid=11235382> [accessed 26 November 2014].

Tomlinson, J. (1991) *Cultural Imperialism: A Critical Introduction*, Baltimore, MD: The Johns Hopkins University Press.

Tunc, T. E. (2007) 'Casablanca: The Romance of Propaganda', *Bright Lights Film Journal*, <http://brightlightsfilm.com/casablanca-romance-propaganda/> [accessed 25 November 2014].

Tweedie, N. (2010) 'The Koh-i-Noor: Diamond robbery?', *The Telegraph*, 29 July, <http://www.telegraph.co.uk/news/features/7917372/The-Koh-i-Noor-diamond-robbery.html> [accessed 26 November 2014].

UK House of Lords, Select Committee on Soft Power and the UK's Influence (2014) 'Persuasion and power in the modern world', Report of Session 2013-14, 28 March, HL Paper 150, <http://www.publications.parliament.uk/pa/ld201314/ldselect/ldsoftpower/150/150.pdf> [accessed 24 November 2014].

UN Security Council (2001) Security Council Resolution 1385 on the situation in Sierra Leone, 19 December, S/RES/1385 (2001), <http://www.un.org/docs/scres/2001/sc2001.htm> [accessed 26 November 2014].

US Department of State (2005) 'Protecting your intellectual property rights (IPR) in China', <http://beijing.usembassy-china.org.cn/protecting_ipr.html> [accessed 25 November 2014].

US Executive Office of the President, Office of the United States Trade Representative (2014) 'The People's Republic of China', US-China Trade Facts, 4 April, <http://www.ustr.gov/countries-regions/china-mongolia-taiwan/peoples-republic-china> [accessed 24 November 2014].

Van Veeren, E. (2009) 'Interrogating *24*: Making sense of US counter-terrorism in the global war on terrorism', *New Political Science*, 31(3): 361-384.

Virunga (2014) film, O. von Einseidel (dir.), <http://www.imdb.com/title/tt3455224/> [accessed 26 November 2014].

War Propaganda (2014) Liddle collection, The University Library, Special Collections, University of Leeds, <http://library.leeds.ac.uk/special-collections-exhibitions-war-propaganda> [accessed 26 November 2014].

Watkins Lang, S. (2007) 'Where do we get "Star Wars"?', *The Eagle*, March, <http://www.smdc.army.mil/2008/Historical/Eagle/WheredowegetStarWars.pdf>, [accessed 25 November 2014].

Weber, C. (2014) *International Relations Theory: A Critical Introduction*, 4th edition, Abingdon and New York: Routledge.

Welch, D. (n.d.) 'Depicting the enemy', British Library, <http://www.bl.uk/world-war-one/articles/depicting-the-enemy> [accessed 24 November 2014].

Weldes, J. (1999) 'Going cultural: *Star Trek*, sate action and popular culture', *Millennium*, 28(1): 117-134.

Weldes, J. (2001) 'Globalisation is science fiction', Millennium, 30(3): 647-667.

Weldes, J. (2003) 'Popular culture, science fiction and world politics: Exploring intertextual relations', in J. Weldes (ed.) *To Seek out New Worlds: Science Fiction and World Politics*, New York: Palgrave Macmillan, 1-27.

West, K. (2005) 'Diamonds from Sierra Leone', song, lyrics available at <http://www.azlyrics.com/lyrics/kanyewest/diamondsfromsierraleoneremix.html> [accessed 25 November 2014].

van Wichelen, S. (2005) '"My dance immoral? *Alhamdulillah* No!" *Dangut* music and gender politics in contemporary Indonesia', in M. I. Franklin (ed.), *Resounding International Relations: On Culture, Music, and Politics*, New York: Palgrave Macmillan, 161-1177.

Zalewski, M. (1995) 'Well, what is the feminist perspective on Bosnia?', *International Affairs*, 71(2): 339-356.

Popular Culture and Political Identity

CONSTANCE DUNCOMBE
AND
ROLAND BLEIKER
UNIVERSITY OF QUEENSLAND

A shocking video depicting the beheading of kidnapped journalist Stephen Sotloff appeared in September 2014, uploaded online by Islamic State (ISIS). Propaganda videos, even those depicting violent death, have meanwhile become a common tool for terrorist organisations. ISIS in particular has relied on such videos to confront a global audience and recruit potential combatants. The Western response to ISIS has been significantly shaped – not to say provoked – by such manifestations of extreme violence. The sensibilities of Western civilisation were so comprehensively incensed by these videos that they managed, almost single-handedly, to throw the Western military machine into action. The only rational response appears to be a complete annihilation of ISIS. But this swift and determined action also silenced discussion of the circumstances surrounding the growth of this terrorist organisation.

A remarkable feature stands out: the ISIS beheading video, 'A Second Message to America', displayed striking parallels with the popular US television series *Homeland*. The style and format is almost identical. *Homeland* starts with a background image of a maze interspersed with rough-cut footage from television, news coverage and official US statements. Fading Arabic subtitles and images of the Middle East oscillate with President Obama stating that 'we must and we will remain vigilant at home and abroad' (De Graaf and Boyle 2014; see also YouTube[1]). The ISIS video, likewise, uses fading Arabic subtitles and special effects to distort the image of President Obama as he declares that 'we will be vigilant and we will be relentless' (De Graaf and Boyle 2014; *Inside Edition* 2014).

Terrorism experts suggest that the visual 'mimicry' of the ISIS videos serves as both a recruitment tool and an attempt to intimidate the American public (De Graaf and Boyle 2014; *Inside Edition* 2014). In either case, the desired emotional impact is one of fear and anxiety. Here too, parallels abound. The disjointed directorial style of the opening sequence of *Homeland* presents the post-9/11 world as one of uncertainty, misinformation and violence – all metaphorically underlined by the mental illness of the show's central character, Carrie. By mirroring the format of those images, the ISIS video plays on the same feelings of doubt to generate a viewer's mistrust in authority, a fear that the US can no longer protect or provide security for its citizens.

How, then, can we understand these links between popular culture and politics? Particularly important, we suggest, is the power of popular culture to shape political identities and the narratives that sustain them. Popular culture unites 'us' through narratives that delineate who 'we' are and what separates 'us' from others. Linking popular culture and political identity is, of course, not new; there is a bourgeoning body of literature that examines the 'popular culture-world politics continuum' (Grayson, Davies and Philpott 2009, p. 156). The consensus here is that popular culture is far more than an escape from

---

[1]   See here: https://www.youtube.com/watch?v=vRRpeGKNP5Y

everyday life, a brief respite from the reality in which 'the political' traditionally takes place. Popular culture has political power precisely because it is so closely intertwined with consumerism.

In this contribution, we aim at showing how popular culture can both entrench and challenge prevailing identities. There is little doubt that popular culture displays a high level of complicity in the power positioning of traditional political and economic orders. Some scholars also stress how political practitioners are influenced by the visual world that television, film, and online media produce (Carver 2010, p. 426). At the same time, much has been made about the role of political leaders and governments in manufacturing the line between fiction and reality through film (see Der Derian 2009; Carver 2010; Dodds 2014; Grayson, Davies and Philpott 2009). The political economy of film is, indeed, intertwined with the needs and desires of political leaders, and yet it also provides the framework within which these needs and desires emerge. But there are also opportunities for dissent and rupture. Film and television, for instance, can offer subversive messages: moments when prevailing identities are challenged and new forms of political narratives emerge. Politics and popular culture are thus co-constituted.

This brings us to the main point we want to make in this short commentary: that this co-constitution is particularly shaped by the role that visuality and emotions play. More attention thus needs to be paid to the visual and emotional dimensions of popular culture, as in the above-mentioned parallels between *Homeland* and the ISIS beheading video. Both are inherently visual phenomena and both are deeply emotional in origin, nature and impact. The axis between visuality and emotions is essential to understanding why ISIS videos created such an immediate and decisive public and political response.

Entrenching Political Identities

Using the example of US national identity, we start by outlining very briefly how popular culture – film and television in particular – can sustain prevailing political narratives. Hollywood is, of course, known to use stereotypes and glorify national values: narratives of national cohesion are visualised in films, and the emotional pull they create for the audience helps to strengthen particular conceptions of identity. However, the issues at stake are, we contend, subtler than this.

Consider the role of 'superheroes' in US popular culture. They can be said to represent stereotypical American values by dramatising the personality traits of rugged individualism, courage, persistence, moral virtue and love of nation (Gabilliet 2010, p. 309; Campbell and Kean 1997, p. 26; Merelman, Streich and Martin 1998, p. 784; Dittmer 2005, p. 633). Captain America is a good example of a popular superhero that embodies US state identity and provides an exalted, idealised figure symbolising the American dream and defending the state structures that make this dream possible (Dittmer 2005, p. 627). His costume – a red, white and blue star-spangled uniform – makes direct reference to the US flag. He represents the 'best aspects of America: courage and honesty' (Dittmer 2005, p. 629). With this comes a broader geopolitical narrative that presents the US as a defensive, not offensive, nation. US moral virtue is reaffirmed through this narrative that presents the US as both a universal model and, at the same time, as peaceful and exceptional. This notion of US exceptionalism and the associated 'us versus them' dynamic is represented in numerous movies: *Captain America* (1990), *Captain America: The First Avenger* (2011), *The Avengers* (2012), *Captain America: Winter Soldier* (2014) (see Dittmer 2005, pp. 629-30).

Television entrenches political identities just as movies do. Look at how the American Ad Council's 'I Am An American'[2] advertising campaign created an emotional connection between audience and nation: a sense of safety and contentment with the nation was then juxtaposed with feeling of fear about 'others'. Launched ten days after the September 11 terrorist attacks, the campaign sought to overcome the anxiety caused by the attacks through narratives of national togetherness (Weber 2010, p. 81). The campaign theme was one of reaching unity through diversity, reflecting the prevailing US identity narrative: a united and harmonious nation is forged out of people from a great number of different ethnic and racial origins. While undoubtedly inclusive on many accounts, such a narrative nevertheless excludes all of those who are not part of the American national unit (Weber 2010, p. 81). By coalescing the diversity of the nation into a single unit, the campaign implicitly suggested togetherness could only be created in opposition to a non-American Other.

Popular culture, then, is political in the most fundamental sense: it creates and entrenches a politics of identity. Representations of who 'we' are engender an emotional response that reinforces a narrative of national togetherness. How we feel about being part of a greater political community, even if we cannot possibly know every single person in it, is both contingent upon and reflected by the images we hold of ourselves and of those around us. Movies and television shows and even television advertising campaigns play an important role in presenting identity such that we feel happiness, pride, and even love for our nation.

Destabilising Political Identities

While undoubtedly entrenching political identities, popular culture can also destabilise and reconstitute these very identities. Here too, we offer only a very short example, taken from the more recent rupture and reassessment of American values in the post-9/11 era.

---

[2]   'I Am An American [Ad Council], YouTube, <https://www.youtube.com/watch?v=vPIXLUrljXg>.

The War on Terror has become a particularly prominent theme in popular culture; consider films such as *Fahrenheit 9/11* (2004), *Syriana* (2005), *The Kingdom* (2007), *Charlie Wilson's War* (2007), *In the Valley of Elah* (2007), *Redacted* (2008), *The Hurt Locker* (2008) and *Zero Dark Thirty* (2012), and television shows like *Homeland* and *Generation Kill*. They all explore and reflect on questions about US behaviour in the War on Terror. They all deal with issues of inclusion and exclusion, of us versus them (Dodds 2008, p. 1621; Philpott 2010, p. 328; Der Derian 2005, p. 34). These visual engagements with 'American values' are reinforced through both media coverage and an increasingly large number of personal films made and circulated through ever more sophisticated and widely available technologies (Philpott 2010, pp. 328-329).

Particularly prominent are visual metaphors associated with Abu Ghraib, Guantanamo Bay and the theatres of war in the Middle East. Images of captive submissiveness, the paternalism of community engagement, and cultural differences confront the viewer as part of the increasing trauma of 'witnessing' the War on Terror. These visual threads also hark back to the earlier mentioned role of the 'superhero'. But he or she now takes on a slightly different role, one that is far more vulnerable than the invincible adventures of Batman and Superman. Look at the new heroes of Jason Bourne in the *Bourne* series, Carrie Mathison in *Homeland*, Jack Bauer in *24*, Bob Barnes in *Syriana* and Maya in *Zero Dark Thirty*. They are all driven by a belief in what America represents. Yet they do not have the boundless energy and optimism of their predecessors. The new heroes are tired, dirty and damaged. They are afflicted by the knowledge of what they have done and what they will have to do to protect America. Jason Bourne's amnesia, Carrie Mathison's bipolar disorder, Bob Barnes' missing fingernails, Maya's tearful emptiness, and even Jack Bauer's lament that 'this is the longest day of my life' are all embodiments on screen of the suffering for and of the American nation. Most importantly, the challenges that these new heroes face are not just the physical challenges that the old superheroes had to encounter and overcome. Our new heroes confront far more difficult personal and emotional demons: the fear, anger, and anxiety of the post-9/11 world is transposed into the very bodies of these compromised heroes. We feel for how these lead characters suffer because we too live in the post 9-11 era and we too experience the associated anxieties.

The new and more complex notion of post-9/11 heroism has significant political consequences. The contours of different political narratives and identities have become more visible. Many film and television renderings of the War on Terror no longer follow the traditional narrative arc of good versus evil. The hero no longer saves the world. The grand finale of the respective films and television shows often raises more questions about the US role in the world than it solves.

Ambiguity has become a key part of both popular culture and the popular response to it. While many viewers reacted positively to the questions brought up in films about the US role and responsibility in the War on Terror, others responded with outrage and hostility. Films such as *Redacted* and *Fahrenheit 9/11*, for instance, were strongly attacked by the influential TV host and commentator Bill O'Reilly, who dismissed the former film as 'vile' and the latter as 'Leni Riefenstahl Third Reich Propaganda' (O'Reilly 2007; Der Derian 2005, p. 34; Philpott 2010, p. 326). The conservative Citizens United even labelled *Fahrenheit 9/11* 'a violation of federal election law' (Der Derian 2005, p. 34; Bronfen 2006, p. 37). These critiques are representative of a wider conservative audience that expected a different response to 9/11, one that should have been more in line with traditional heroic narratives that categorically defend and justify 'American values'. Here, our new and more fragile heroes are met mostly with anger, disbelief, and resentment – reminding us that the seemingly homogenous American identity is much more fractured and delicate than the uniform certainty that was upheld in traditional popular culture narratives.

In short, popular culture can engender positive emotional responses that trigger feelings of national togetherness. But it can do the opposite, too; film and television can destabilise the security of identity and evoke a confused or weakened state. Suggesting that foreign policy behaviour is not quite as honourable or exceptional as previously thought can produce feelings of anger, anxiety, and insecurity. Disbelief is an inevitable first reaction to narratives that contradict long-held stories told about past and present behaviour. However, these forms of popular destabilisations are also essential to debates about reassessing and reconstituting identities in the wake of traumatic experiences, such as the terrorist attacks of 9/11.

Challenging Political Identities

We now take one further step and illustrate how non-Western popular cultures resist and challenge prevailing identities. Rather than being set up in opposition to traditional filmmaking style, non-Western movies often follow a similar narrative structure. However, this structure is then used to present a narrative of resistance to hegemonic Western discourses about the non-West. A key part of this narrative strategy is emotions, in particular shame and resentment, humiliation and love.

Feelings of shame and resentment about Western dismissals of particular non-Western identities are frequently explored through film and television, particularly in terms of triumphing over these emotions to reassert identity. One good example of resistance to dominant identity frames and the emotional context of shame on which it is built can be found in the popular Turkish film *Valley of the Wolves*, which follows the formula of a Hollywood action thriller. The film images a confrontation between a Turkish secret agent and a US officer responsible for capturing Turkish forces in northern Iraq, visually representing a similarly 'deeply resented incident' between US and Turkish forces in 2003 (Dodds 2008, p. 1623). The key difference between it and Hollywood action-thriller films, however, is that instead of the heroic US agent battling against a violent foe, the film relies on the reversal of those roles and it is the Turkish secret agent who triumphs (Dodds 2008, pp. 1623-1624). The film visualises the Turkish experience of overcoming shame in the face of a greater US power. Turkish identity is then positively reconstituted through visually defeating feelings of shame and resentment that had been tied to US-Turkish relations.

The non-West resistance to Western identity narratives is narrated through a triumph over the feelings of humiliation. Bollywood films are a good example of this dynamic: visual representations of India and Indians are used to explore the return to modern-traditional values and the rejection of both Western lifestyles and Western representations of India that are often demeaning (Kaur 2002, p. 207). Popular film *Kuch Kuch Hota Hai* (1998) explored these themes of absence and return through a romantic comedy storyline that some suggested was a 'Hollywood clone, except that the actors were Indian' (Kaur 2002, p. 208). While the genre fit the generalised parameters of a rom com, much like *Valley of the Wolves* fit the action thriller genre, the importance of films such as *Kuch Kuch Hota Hai* is the emotional connection to the visual representations on screen. While Western visual representations of India – most often involving mysticism, famine, drought or, more recently, call centres – can elicit feelings of humiliation, the Bollywood images of India inspire a positive affect relating to a sense of pride in how India and its values and traditions are being portrayed in film (Kaur 2002, p. 208).

Love is another emotion that is used to explore non-Western identity narratives challenging hegemonic Western discourses. This is particularly the case in South Korean films that deal with the topic of political crises surrounding the North-South Korea divide. While Western films generally portray North Korea as an irrational, brutal, poverty-stricken security problem to be 'solved' by South Korea and the international community (Choi 2013, p. 1), some South Korean films have explored this political dynamic through the emotional context of love. The emotive narrative of love – togetherness, intimacy, conquering all – as part of the drive towards national unification is evident not only within popular films such as *Shiri* (1999) and *JSA* (2000) but also as a political practice in its own right (Choi 2013, pp. 1-2). South Korean policy towards the North is thus imbued with emotion that both extends from and is reflected in the politicised visual representations inherent in Korean popular culture.

Conclusion: The Crucial Role of Images and Emotions

Popular culture matters to world politics. It is a significant identity marker that tells us who we are and how we should feel about both 'us' and 'them'. Drawing on an increasingly bourgeoning and sophisticated body of literature, we have highlighted how film and television shows can entrench political identities, but we also pointed out how popular culture can destabilise and even challenge these identities.

The co-constituted relationship between popular culture and political identity hinges on two particularly crucial features: the powerful visual dimensions of film and television, and the inherently emotional reactions they trigger. Popular culture is, to a large degree, visual culture, and it has a strong affective component that arises through people's experience of positive and negative representations of their identity.

More work thus needs to be done on how the politics of popular culture interacts with visual and emotional factors. There is, meanwhile, an extensive body of literature on both visual politics and on the links between emotions and politics – so much so that we cannot even begin to list, yet alone summarise, the respective contributions. There is something inherently unique about the visual part of popular culture. Images – still or moving – work differently to words. That is their very nature. They are visceral. They evoke strong reactions in viewers. And a big part of these reactions is of an emotional nature. The shocking nature of the ISIS videos – as well as their political significance – cannot be appreciated without understanding their visual nature and the deeply emotional impact they have. Likewise, films and television shows that deal with war and identity do so through images that are intensely emotional and create intensely emotional reactions and attachments in viewers. Images and emotions are, indeed, everywhere in politics, and yet they have only recently become a serious and systematic topic of investigation. This is why the political study of popular culture would profit greatly from a more sustained engagement with these debates that deal with both images and emotions.

References

Åhäll, L. (2009) 'Images, Popular Culture, Aesthetics, Emotions: The Future of International Politics?', *Political Perspectives*, 3(1): 1-44.

Bronfen, E. (2006) 'Reality check: image affects and cultural memory', *differences*, 17(1): 20-46.

Campbell, N. and A. Kean. (1997) *American Cultural Studies: An Introduction to American Culture*, London: Routledge.

Carver, T. (2010) 'Cinematic ontologies and viewer epistemologies: knowing international politics as moving images', *Global Society*, 24(3): 421-431.

Chen, B., C. C. Hwang and L. H. M. Ling (2009) 'Lust/caution in IR: democratising world politics with culture as a method', *Millennium: Journal of International Studies*, 37(3): 743-766.

Choi, S. (2013) 'Love's cruel promises: Love, unity and North Korea', *International Feminist Journal of Politics* (ahead of print): 1-18.

De Graaf, M. and S. Boyle (2014) 'Was ISIS hostage video inspired by Homeland's opening credits? Expert reveals how themes from popular culture are used to attract Western recruits', *The Daily Mail Online*, 4 September 2014, <http://www.dailymail.co.uk/news/article-2742248/Is-ISIS-copying-Hollywood-drama-techniques-recruit-young-disaffected-westerners-Jihad.html#ixzz3HhtlDITL> [accessed 30 October 30 2014].

Der Derian, J. (2005) 'Imaging terror: logos, pathos and ethos', *Third World Quarterly*, 26(1): 23-37.

Dittmer, J. (2005) 'Captain America's Empire: Reflections on Identity, Popular Culture, and Post-9/11 Geopolitics', *Annals of the Association of American Geographers*, 95(3): 626-643.

Dodds, K. (2014) 'Popular Geopolitics and the War on Terror', *E-International Relations*, this issue.

Dodds, K. (2008) '"Have You Seen Any Good Films Lately?" Geopolitics, International Relations and Film', *Geography Compass*, 2(2): 476-494.

Gabilliet, J. (2010) *Of Comics and Men: A Cultural History of American Comic Books*, B. Beaty and N. Nguyen (trans.), Jackson, Mississippi: University Press of Mississippi.

Grayson, K., M. Davies and S. Philpott (2009) 'Pop Goes IR? Researching the Popular Culture–World Politics Continuum', *Politics*, 29(3): 155-163.

Inside Edition (2014) 'Is ISIS Using "Homeland" to Recruit Terrorists?', 4 September 2014, <http://www.insideedition.com/headlines/8864-is-isis-using-homeland-to-recruit-terrorists> [accessed on 30 October 2014].

Kaur, R. (2002) 'Viewing the West through Bollywood: A celluloid Occident in the making', *Contemporary South Asia*, 11(2): 199-209.

Merelman, R. M., G. Streich and P. Martin (1998) 'Unity and diversity in American political culture: An exploratory study of the National Conversation on American Pluralism and Identity', *Political Psychology*, 19(4): 781-807.

Philpott, S. (2010) 'Is anyone watching? War, cinema and bearing witness', *Cambridge Review of International Affairs*, 23(2): 325-348.

O'Reilly, B. (2007) 'Harming America the Pop Culture Way...', *Fox News*, 6 November, <http://www.foxnews.com/story/2007/11/06/harming-america-pop-culture-way/> [accessed 13 November 2014].

Weber, C. (2006) 'An aesthetics of fear: the 7/7 London bombings, the sublime, and werenotafraid.com', *Millennium: Journal of International Studies*, 34(3): 683-711.

Weber, C. (2010) 'Citizenship, security, humanity', *International Political Sociology*, 4(1): 80-85.

On *Captain America* and 'Doing' Popular Culture in the Social Sciences

JASON DITTMER
UNIVERSITY COLLEGE LONDON

Prelude

I didn't know I was going to end up the 'comic book guy'[1] of political geography. I started off quite respectable, really, looking at the news media as a space in which processes such as NATO and EU expansion were not only represented but also worked out discursively. A bit constructivist, maybe, but at least I was looking at high politics and broadsheet newspapers. I mean, everyone knows the importance of news media in the framing of politics. Sure, it didn't have obvious policy relevance, but when someone at a cocktail party asked me what I did, I could hold my head high. 'NATO expansion,' I would say, and heads would nod sagely. This was 'real' work, validated by almost every cocktail party and academic conference I went to.

Of course, as with every slippery slope, it is hard to pinpoint when I started down my path. You only notice when you're incapable of going back. My gateway drug was teaching. Sure, I could *tell* students about the social construction of regions like Eastern Europe, identifying the competing discourses with reference to the tables found in my dissertation. Or, I could *show* them *Bram Stoker's Dracula* (1992), and then lead a discussion about the portrayal of West and East in the film. While this was obviously a sordid excuse to show a movie in class, I promised myself that I would elevate the discussion through my own insights into the original novel. Even then I knew that some forms of popular culture were more respectable than others.[2] Lo and behold, talking to students about political geography through pop culture actually produced better results (Dittmer 2006).

'That was great,' I thought to myself. 'I should do more of that.' So I threw myself into my new project, a study of *Captain America* comics from 1940 to the present. 'I'll do this for a year and then write a book about it,' I remember thinking. It ballooned to include other nationalist superheroes from the UK and Canada, went down a different theoretical path and took ten years rather than one, but otherwise I totally called it (Dittmer 2013). Inspired by scholars such as Klaus Dodds (also featured in this Edited Collection) and his work on the geopolitics of political cartoons and the *James Bond* films, I knew there was a literature to which my work could speak and draw from. When my first attempt on the subject was accepted in one of the top journals in geography (Dittmer 2005), I knew I was onto something. I smugly submitted the abstract to a conference and prepared myself for praise.

At the conference, I stood up and started outlining the geopolitical significance of Captain America in the post-11 September 2001 era. As I got a few minutes in, I saw some meaningful looks shared between some of the senior professors sitting in the front rows. A

---

[1]   https://socialvirion.files.wordpress.com/2011/11/comic_book_guy1.jpg.

[2]   'The Geek Hierarchy', <http://3.bp.blogspot.com/_29_shKT4Elw/R1L0LSjRtsI/AAAAAAAACSo/
      J5mUYyrb-y4/s1600-R/geeks.gif>.

few minutes later, there was outright laughter – and not at my *bon mot* about Captain America's pirate boots.[3] It was the kind you don't want during your presentation: derisive laughter. It was my first experience of the Foucauldian meaning of 'academic discipline' – the internalisation of academic norms in ways that shape subsequent behaviour. To be clear, this was my worst ever experience of this type, and in general I have had very positive responses. I attribute this largely to the generosity of scholars in geography: it is a remarkably open-minded and inclusive discipline. But how was I to reconcile this negative experience with my publication success? It was then that I realised that the academy had a schizophrenic relationship with popular culture. It was clearly important, because we swim in a sea of popular culture. Yet it was also ubiquitous, and therefore debased. Understanding this tension is, I think, central to 'doing' pop culture studies in the social sciences.

Conceptualising Popular Culture in IR

The social sciences in general have a tendency to privilege the big, the macro and the structural. This has, until now, been especially true of international relations and political geography, which have sought macro-scaled generalisations that explain the empirical patterns seemingly evident around us. This is why few scholars have a problem saying that popular culture matters. Of course it matters; how else could we scapegoat it for society's ills? The problem of course is that popular culture is an umbrella term for so many things, from media objects (like *Captain America* or *The Hunger Games*) to games we play (whether sports, board games, or *Candy Crush*), to social networking (Twitter, Facebook, Instagram, etc.), that when you focus in on a single element of popular culture, it feels *petty*. How could Captain America be really responsible for anything, good or bad, in global politics?

In truth, I agree. The problem lies in our conceptualisation of popular culture as a *thing*: an object that can be grasped, considered and analysed. This was one problem with my original idea for my Captain America study. All I thought I had to do was read all the comics and render my verdict. Rather, popular culture is a *doing*. It is what we do, in common, with others. This liveliness is what is lost when popular culture is reduced to a thing. Captain America is not just the comics with his name on them, rather, he is the multiplicity of forms that proliferate around that signifier as people read, write, draw, talk about, think about and generally live with Captain America in their world (thankfully I finished the book before the *Captain America* movies started coming out, or else I would still be working). For this reason, in my study I had to take into account (imperfectly) a wide range of sites, processes and moments: not only the writers of Captain America and their creative acts,

---

[3]   Harris, Sonia (2013) 'Jack Kirby's Captain America pirate boots', Comic Book Resources, < http://goodcomics.comicbookresources.com/2013/02/20/committed-10-great-superhero-boots/6/>.

but also the political economy of comics publishing over time, the various audiences that made sense of these comics, the British and Canadian localisations of the Captain America archetype, the differing political economies and traditions of the British and Canadian comics scenes, the larger narratives and orientations towards nationalism in all three countries, and so on. Captain America emerges via the dynamic interaction of all these things/places/times, rather than as a discrete thing. Any attempt to focus in on one element – for instance, creators' intent or my own reading of the comic – imputes too much power to that one element. Rather, it is the entire assemblage that produces effects.

A lot of the worst scholarship on popular culture and IR/geopolitics starts from a desire to validate the scholar's own interest in the material. Of course there is nothing wrong with having an affection of some sort for the subject material; indeed, I hope for your sake that you do. Another version of the worst scholarship is critique shorn of any understanding of why people might like, for instance, superheroes. Intuiting the attraction to popular culture is a crucial corrective to this all too common perspective. But, paradoxically, both the need to validate *and* the need to critique often turn into a need to inflate, to impute power. It is here that the scholar's urge to look at the macro (to take one random example, the entire run of *Captain America* from 1940 to the present) can be counterproductive. Few non-scholars would do anything so Sisyphean, so how useful is any analysis of this macro-discourse? Rather, the key aspect of thinking through popular culture as assemblage is, in my opinion, to consider the ways in which the popular culture assemblage 'leaks' into other aspects of political life. This requires not a 'completist' macro-sensibility but a willingness to see the macro as emerging from the myriad baroque micro-interactions between creators, artefacts, audiences and those who re-appropriate and re-create from pop culture artefacts (Allen 2003; Jenkins 2012). It is in these lively relationships that the power of popular culture can be found.

'Doing' Popular Culture in IR

Cultivating this sensibility towards popular culture research in IR means turning attention to new sites of research, new concepts and new notions of the political. One such move means focusing less on singular, specific pop culture forms in favour of clusters of related forms that work in assemblage with one another. As I said earlier, popular culture is about doings, about lively interactions between people, pop culture artefacts and the wider world of politics. It is these interactions that ought to be the focus of attention, rather than a single kind of popular culture, no matter how salient it seems. It is for this reason that my project became less about Captain America and more about nationalist superheroes as a way of narrating geopolitics. By doing so, I could not only trace the connections between creators, audiences and contemporary political issues, but also follow the circulation of the nationalist superhero archetype from the US to Canada and the UK, and track the ongoing interactions between them. These connections ought to be traced as carefully as possible, rather than assumed to exist. A range of spaces of interaction have become popular in research, from conventions to social media to specialist web forums.

Further, the materialisations of popular culture are important for several reasons. First, there is, of course, the archive – whether a literal archive, or the encoding of a digital media object (like a DVD or hard drive), or something else. Second, there is the materialisation of popular culture in other forms that persist through time – notably the human body. The human body emerges as important because not only do traces of popular culture materialise in the body – a somatic archive of sorts – but also because the body serves as a site of affective interaction, where new forms of popular culture interact with previous ones, *and* with experiences of current events, as resources for political subject formation (Massumi 2002; Protevi 2009).

This focus on the body points us to the need for new conceptualisations of the political, and terms to help account for them. The frequently heard refrain from the 11 September 2001 attacks, that 'it was like watching a movie,' illustrates how the human body, and its cognitive sense-making abilities, are shaped by ongoing engagements with particular ways of seeing/knowing embedded in popular cultural forms and with the generic forms of narration that accompany those forms. Of course, this capability was latent within the bodies of New Yorkers, activated by the events of the day. This indicates how our bodies may carry within them all sorts of political capabilities that are entirely virtual, or latent. All of this is to say that popular culture does not determine who we think we are, who we think the enemy is, or how we will react in a crisis. Rather, popular culture provides many different sets of resources that *may* be activated under appropriate circumstances. It is a set of capabilities, or lines of flight, that are powerfully world-shaping, but not powerful in the traditional sense. Getting comfortable with that is a key part of moving past the power of the macro, and embracing the power of the baroque.

The laughter at that conference, and the denial of legitimacy it entailed, is not inherent to the study of popular culture. Rather, it is inherent in a particular view of power as something localisable in certain sites or structures, like the state. International Relations and political geography have both traditionally disciplined their subjects to look at those sites or structures and to assume the rest is beneath notice. When scholars of popular culture try to match the grandiosity of that vision of power, the objects they study fail to pass muster. Paradoxically, it is by looking at the diffuse and interacting sites of popular culture – the body, the artefact, the hashtagged Twitter discussion, the archive, and so on – that the enlivening power of popular culture emerges. It is all the more important, and legitimate, for it.

References

Allen, J. (2003) *Lost Geographies of Power*, London: Wiley-Blackwell.

Dittmer, J. (2005) 'Captain America's Empire: Reflections on identity, popular culture, and post-9/11 geopolitics', *Annals of the Association of American Geographers*, 95(3): 626-643.

Dittmer, J. (2006) 'Teaching the social construction of regions in Regional Geography courses; or, why do vampires come from Eastern Europe?', *Journal of Geography in Higher Education*, 30(1): 49-61.

Dittmer, J. (2013) *Captain America and the Nationalist Superhero: Metaphors, Narratives, and Geopolitics*, Philadelphia: Temple University Press.

Dodds, K. (2006) 'Popular geopolitics and audience dispositions: James Bond and the Internet Movie Database (IMDb)', *Transactions of the Institute of British Geographers*, 31(2): 116-130.

Dodds, K. (2007) 'Steve Bell's Eye: Cartoons, geopolitics and the visualization of the "War on Terror"', *Security Dialogue*, 38(2): 157-177.

Jenkins, H. (2012) *Textual Poachers: Television Fans and Participatory Culture, 2nd edition*, London: Routledge.

Massumi, B. (2002) *Parables for the Virtual: Movement, Affect, Sensation*, Durham, NC: Duke University Press.

Protevi, J. (2009) *Political Affect*, Minneapolis: University of Minnesota Press.

Popular Geopolitics and War on Terror

KLAUS DODDS
ROYAL HOLLOWAY, UNIVERSITY OF LONDON

Within weeks of President George W. Bush announcing that the United States and its allies would initiate a 'War on Terror', academics and journalists were reflecting and speculating on what role the entertainment industry and popular culture might play in this enterprise. In November 2011, for example, a widely reported 'Beverly Hills Summit' was held in which it was suggested that representatives from film and television companies offered their assistance to presidential special advisor, Karl Rove (cited in Stockwell 2005). This 'offer', historically speaking, was not unusual in the sense that there is a long record of Hollywood acting (see Robb 2004), producing and promoting films either supportive of the United States and its material and ideational interests or collaborating closely with government departments such as Defense and the CIA on particular film projects (e.g. *The Longest Day* [1961] and *Animal Farm* [1954], respectively).

In the past, presidents, such as ex-Hollywood actor Ronald Reagan, appeared to understand that Cold War geopolitics could be assembled and reproduced in filmic terms. When President Reagan described the Soviet Union as the 'evil empire' in 1983, commentators were swift to detect thinly disguised parallels with the *Star Wars* franchise. The Soviet leadership as proverbial 'Darth Vaders' and their armed forces represented as latter-day storm troopers (however awkward, given heavy Soviet losses against Nazi German forces in the Second World War) appeared to fit comfortably with a presidential narrative littered with references to 'freedom', 'forces of evil', and a 'struggle' for the future of the world. And to cap it all, a so-called Strategic Defence Initiative (involving a space-based weapons system) was termed 'star wars'. Reagan's dress, speech and demeanor were attuned and attentive to popular cultural references. He dressed and acted the part of statesman, cowboy, commander in chief and folksy everyday man. He quoted lines from Clint Eastwood movies and other films, including *Rambo: First Blood* (1982). Films such as *Missing in Action* (1984) and *Top Gun* (1986) can be identified as the archetypical Reagan movie fantasy – young, white, muscular, heterosexual American men (and all those characteristics matter) flying their technologically sophisticated planes and shooting down enemy pilots and/or rescuing missing Vietnam POWs.

When, in May 2003, President George W. Bush piloted a plane and landed on the flight deck of an aircraft carrier, observers noted striking similarities with *Top Gun* (for a good summary, see Rich 2007). One reading of *Top Gun* and its ilk is that the 1980s techno-thriller was a popular geopolitical response to the humiliation of the 'failure' of Vietnam in the 1960s and 1970s. Unable to defeat Vietcong forces in the jungles of South East Asia, these films and their actors with their 'hard bodies' (as Susan Jeffords 1994 noted many years ago) perform a redemptive role – a new generation of men battling and overcoming adversaries in new places such as the Middle East, the Indian Ocean, Central Asia, and even South East Asia. After posing in his flying suit, President Bush changed into his dark suit and announced that combat operations were complete in Iraq, following an invasion in March 2003. Even if his pronouncement proved to be rather over-optimistic, the stagecraft and statecraft were intriguing; his landing and performance were timed to coincide with peak TV news hours and the aircraft carrier in question was stationed off the Californian coastline. And to add extra zest, a banner with 'mission accomplished' was hung from the control tower of the aircraft carrier.

So far, we have two themes running through this introduction – first, presidents and governments have encouraged a close relationship with public entertainment industries. Governments facilitate, fund and at times discipline producers of film, radio, television programmes. There is a political economy to the movie business, and writers such as James Der Derian (2009) have spoken of the military-industrial-media-entertainment network. Hollywood producers, writers and actors who bore the brunt of Cold War 'Red Scares' in the 1940s and 1950s could affirm the disciplinary role of the federal government, as they were humiliated, jailed and harassed for 'anti-American' activities (Robb 2004, Fattor 2014). But governments have also worked closely with the entertainment industry to produce and circulate sponsored films, television programmes and latterly video games (e.g. *America's Army*). More recently, states and governments can and do block internet search engines and monitor and regulate content of all sorts. Second, as our *Top Gun* example suggests, geopolitics might be understood in a more co-constitutive role; so rather than simply regarding popular culture including film as 'reflecting' or 'representing' the real-world of Cold War geopolitics, we might see it as having a more co-productive role. Should we think of the US invasion of Iraq in March 2003 as a quasi-war movie, and the then search and later killing of Osama Bin Laden as a 'quest' movie? And as scholars of film in particular understand, genre brings with it rules, norms and expectations in terms of characterisation, narrative arc and denouement.

What follows is a brief exposition of some of the intellectual underpinnings of this interest in how popular culture and world politics constitute one another. Relevant literature in critical geopolitics and IR is noted, as the article explores three themes that address this overarching concern, namely the representational logics of popular cultural texts, the emotional and affect-laden qualities of popular culture, and the intertextuality of sources. Finally, a brief mention is made of audience consumption and the varied ways in which texts are engaged with.

Popular Geopolitics

Over the last two decades, geopolitics has undergone a substantive transformation and a new academic field called 'critical geopolitics' has consolidated itself in the discipline of Geography and beyond. Strikingly, some of this literature bears similarities with a parallel endeavour in International Relations (IR) to explore, in particular, the relationship between popular culture and world politics (for example, Bleiker 2001, Weber 2006, Shepherd 2013). More recently, these strands have been brought into conversation with one another, and journals such as *Critical Studies on Security, E-IR, Geopolitics and Political Geography* have been important sites for these intellectual encounters. Recent articles by David Grondin (2014),[1] Matt Davies (2013)[2] and Cahir Doherty (2013)[3] convey well some of the debates and even controversies regarding IR's engagement with popular culture.

Popular geopolitics owes a great deal to the pioneering work of political geographer Joanne Sharp – in particular, her study of *Reader's Digest* and the ways it constructed the Cold War Soviet Union as 'Other' (Sharp 2000). By focusing on the textual and visual elements of this monthly magazine, she considered how the Soviet Union was conceptualised as a particular kind of place governed by a series of Communist Party-led regimes, intent on spatial expansionism, the domination of place and ideological struggle across the globe. Much of the subsequent work, especially in the 1990s, was tackling the absolute neglect in traditional geopolitical research of the popular and the everyday. A distinction was drawn between what was termed the formal geopolitical reasoning and practices of academics, the practical geopolitics of governments and political leaders, and the popular geopolitics to be found in media outlets such as film and television. What dominated research proceedings was an interest in speeches and textual sources, with an abiding concern for how popular geopolitical sources ended up naturalising and legitimising the practical geopolitical narratives and identities of governments such as the United States.

Later work, mostly informed by feminist geopolitical scholarship (e.g. Weber 2006 and Shepherd 2013), has critiqued this focus on the textual and media sources such as Hollywood films and video games. Instead, emphasis was placed on other registers such as the everyday, the local, the household, the embodied, and the politics of emotion such as fear and hope (Moore and Shepherd 2010). This has encouraged a new generation of scholars in the 2000s onwards to re-direct the attention of popular geopolitics away from an interest in textual analysis per se towards a vein of research concerned with how individuals and communities are embedded and affected by geopolitical sites, relations, objects and networks (Dodds, Kuus, and Sharp 2013). Some of this might appear banal, mundane and barely noticed, but as some feminist scholars note, the declaration of a war on terror had profoundly different consequences for people depending on class, gender, race, sexuality, and so on (Puar 2007). A popular geopolitics of the war on terror would take account of the embodied experiences and the manner in which emotions such as fear

---

[1]   Grondin, D. (2014) 'Publicizing the US National Security State through Entertainment', E-International Relations, <http://www.e-ir.info/2014/08/06/publicizing-the-us-national-security-state-through-entertainment>.

[2]   Davies, M. (2013) 'Teaching IR with Popular Culture', E-International Relations, <http://www.e-ir.info/2013/06/26/teaching-ir-with-popular-culture/>.

[3]   O'Doherty, C. (2013) 'Pop Culture, huh, What Is It Good For? A Lot of Things, Actually', E-International Relations, <http://www.e-ir.info/2013/10/25/pop-culture-huh-what-is-it-good-for-a-lot-of-things-actually/>.

have played in the past, and continue to play in the present, a vital role in creating and sustaining what we might call 'popular geopolitical atmospheres', in which some people are judged to be more suspicious, more dangerous and more worrisome than others. Popular sources such as film and television still play an important role in feeding and nourishing those geopolitical atmospheres and anxieties.

Televising and Filming the War on Terror

The 9/11 assault on New York and Washington DC, and even the ill-fated United 93 aircraft which crashed in Pennsylvania, proved to be fertile ground for popular cultural debates and interventions. The sheer scale of human loss and physical destruction on the one hand and the public declaration of intent by the United States government to destroy those responsible on the other hand proved irresistible. Highly televised, the co-constitutive nature of the 'attacks' started with citizens and journalists making references to disaster movies (Weber 2010), suggesting, in an uncanny sort of way, that cinema-watching audiences had witnessed such destruction before, especially in New York City. But unlike some of those disaster movies from the 1970s and even the 1990s, many of those trapped in the Twin Towers were not going to be rescued by fire fighters and police officers (see the Oliver Stone movie *World Trade Center* [2006]).

Such popular cultural references to the 'disaster movie' (Keane 2006), however, offer us an entry point into how movies and television programmes provide a source for interrogating the production and consumption of popular geopolitics (Carter and Dodds 2014). We might distinguish three aspects to this task: first, how do the representational logics of films operate with regard to depiction of places, people and politics? Are there dominant threads to be detected, such as how enemies are represented or the manner in which certain places are judged to be safe, dangerous, unstable, hellish, and so on? Second, how do films or other media outlets amplify affect during and after their release? We might be interested in the way in which films and other media contribute to a cultural politics of fear, hope, despair, pride, resurgence, and so on. Third, how might a film or television program be interpreted in relation to other popular cultural texts and world politics/affairs? While I will concentrate on these three aforementioned items, it is clearly possible to add a fourth, which revolves around audiences and their consumptive practices, and I touch a little on that later on in the article. In other words, how and in what ways do people consume, engage in and even ignore such media?

Representational Logics

The representational logics of film and television do matter, especially if there is a recurrent pattern of depicting some places, ideas and communities as deviant and dangerous and some others as righteous and legitimate. Some generic film types proved very popular at the cinema with audiences. Post 9/11, the superhero film rose in popularity as figures such as Batman and Superman, not to mention others such as Iron Man and Captain America, enjoyed positive box office returns (Dittmer 2011, Adey 2013). Interestingly, despite their popularity in the main, films such as *Man of Steel* (2013) were accused of trading in 'disaster porn' (Chang and Debruge 2013), capitalising on the visual imagery associated with urban destruction and the resulting fear that engulfed those who witnessed events in New York either in person or via television cameras.

Perhaps the format of the standard Hollywood film is not the right place to offer such nuance. The television series *Homeland* (2011–present) is an acclaimed serial drama, which considers how the eventual return of a male US marine sergeant and the work of a female CIA agent coincide. It has been widely lauded for its complex and multi-layered story format. What drives the basic narrative forward is the realisation that the returning soldier might actually be a terrorist who has been 'turned' by Al-Qaeda operatives during his long period in captivity. As the series unfolds, the narrative arc and the development of characters depend on a series of place-based depictions shaped by axes of gender, sexuality and race (for a brief reflection, see Zalewski 2013). It matters, for instance, that Sergeant Nicholas Brody, the returning marine, had a family living in suburban America. Brody's household, while at times dysfunctional, represents a hetero-normative ideal of nuclear family (Puar 2007). This contrasts strongly with the fleeting references to Iraq, the Lebanon and Afghanistan, which are depicted as chaotic, noisy, dusty and seemingly far removed from the suburban civility of the United States.

Homeland has been credited with being insightful with regards to the politics of surveillance, the fragile distinction between 'terrorist' and 'patriot', and the difficulty of pursuing the war on terror in the face of multiple sources of field-based and signals-led 'intelligence'. The serial narrative format allows for characters to be more richly depicted than in a film format, and, as a consequence, the depiction of friends and enemies within and beyond the CIA is complicated. As part of that complexity, it is also a deeply geographical serial drama, which suggests that the war on terror has an everyday quality to it, as CIA agents normalise the monitoring of the Brody family and try to ascertain whether Brody himself is actually a terrorist plotting to assassinate the president or a serving Congressional representative recovering from post-traumatic stress. The bedroom, living room, car, café and public square all become implicated in an ongoing operation led by CIA agents designed to scrutinise every aspect of his life. The impact on his family and military colleagues is shown to be deeply stressful and traumatic for the family members, as the war on terror is keenly felt on the home front too.

Other highly regarded serial dramas such as *The Wire* (2002–2008) also demonstrate well how the popular geopolitics of war on terror can challenge and unsettle dominant representational logics, especially those focusing on a simplistic distinction between a home front and dangerous others in places like Afghanistan, Iraq and Yemen. By focusing on the everyday lives of criminals, police officers, city officials and others in Baltimore, the series suggests that the war on drugs and the war on terror shared something in common, especially in the area of surveillance. Whether attention was devoted to drug supplies or terror networks, police officers in particular resort to increasingly desperate, even exceptional, measures to disrupt those people, places and objects involved in drugs and terror operations. But the everyday consequences of such activities are disproportional in the sense of touching the lives of the poorest, ethnic minorities and others who exist on the proverbial margins of Baltimore's economy.

Affect

How might film and other popular media be caught up in what has been termed affective economies? Here we might consider not only the manner in which the film is amplified and intensified through affect, but also how we as viewers might be affected by a combination of lighting, dress, places and demeanour. To give an example, the film *Frozen River* (2008) is a story about two women (a white working-class mother and a single Mohawk Indian mother) brought together by freakish circumstances, which lead to them getting involved in an illegal people-smuggling operation. The movie opens with a lingering late winter shot of the gloomy and frozen St Lawrence River (the smuggling route from Canada to the United States), and the camera later lingers on the thin body and worn clothing of the white woman (named Ray) living in a decrepit mobile home in the US-Canadian borderlands. Almost immediately, as a viewer I felt sympathy, even pity, for her everyday life as she struggled to raise two children with little money and a husband who, we later discover, is a gambler. The presence of snow and ice only seem to further emphasise her precarious life (for a longer review, see Dodds 2013).

The filming and narrative arc of *Frozen River* invites, perhaps even elicits, affect, as we discover how Ray and her Mohawk Indian companion Lila seek to avoid arrest by police officers and violence from rival smugglers. The film generates subjectivity – we want, as viewers, to witness Ray and Lila's endurance, and are moved by their everyday struggles to combat poverty and, in Lila's case, racism and discrimination, against a backdrop of greater political anxieties about border security. In one poignant moment in the film, in the claustrophobic environment of their little car parked in the middle of the St Lawrence River late one night, one of the bags of a young Pakistani couple they have hidden in the back of their car becomes an object of suspicion. Ray decides that the bag is a security risk and dumps it on the frozen river. Later, she discovers to her evident horror that the bag contained a baby. The subsequent search for the bag is all the more affecting when we see the two women driving desperately in search of the bag in near darkness, save for the headlights of the vehicle.

While a distinction is made by scholars such as Brian Massumi (2002) between affect (the primary, pre-subjective intensive) and emotion (the conscious, descriptive and meaningful), film scholars and others interested in other media such as video games are drawing attention to how we might think about what it *feels* ('structures of feeling') like, for example, to be a poor white working-class woman or a Pakistani immigrant trying to negotiate the border security regimes of the United States and Canada. What makes *Frozen River* fascinating is the manner in which the border itself is shown to be intensely material (the snow and ice make it possible to cross the river boundary illegally) and complex in the sense that there is a Mohawk reservation, which lies across both the Canadian and American sides of the St Lawrence River. Tribal sovereignty co-exists with US and Canadian state sovereignty, and this creates opportunities for Mohawk women such as Lila to engage in smuggling operations that bypass the formal border controls between the two countries.

More generally, what the film achieves is to show how seemingly abstract notions such as the war on terror and neo-liberal globalisation find expression in the everyday lives of those living in the borderlands. What *Frozen River* does is show both the *effects* of heightened border security (e.g. border patrols, border posts, identity checks) and the *affects* of neoliberal globalisation and the war on terror (Dodds 2013). In Ray's case, her financial desperation drives her (literally) to take ever-greater risks as she endures the humiliation of struggling to give her children enough money to cover their school lunches. She worries every time a police officer gives her a passing glance and, as Lila tells her, this sense of being watched and evaluated is worse for her as a Mohawk Indian. The film does not appear to have the time or space to explore how you might feel to be trapped in the boot of a car and then trusting someone else to transport you across a frozen river to a place where you cannot possibly have much sense of what it might be like on arrival.

Intertextuality

The final area of interest is how films and television series might be understood alongside other popular cultural texts. The term 'intertextuality' highlights how each text exists in relation to others. Some texts, such as the *James Bond* film series, deliberately and knowingly connect with one another – indeed, the overlaps are considered an important part of audience pleasure, especially for fans. So audiences watching *Skyfall* (2012), for example, would have had the opportunity to detect allusions to other Bond films stretching all the way back to *Dr. No* (1962). Such allusions include the character of Bond as spy, his relationship with women, the role and significance of technology and gadgets, the use of violence and its connection to mission completion, and finally, the role of sites and spaces (e.g. M's office and 'exotic' locations such as Brazil, Egypt and Thailand).

Skyfall (2012), the third film starring Daniel Craig as James Bond, is profoundly intertextual, as audiences discover that the Skyfall is Bond's childhood home in Scotland. As Bond and M battle against a disgruntled former MI6 agent intent on terrorising London and MI6 itself, audiences are given insights into his childhood, especially in the aftermath of the death of his parents. The film is intensely geopolitical in the manner in which it reflects upon the relationship between terror, cyber-espionage and Britain's role in the world. Right at the start of the film, the focus is on tracking down a disc encrypted with secret information about UK spies. Bond's quest is both physical and virtual, however. He needs to recover the top-secret disk while at the same time he struggles to discover how the villain has cyber-hacked into MI6's computer networks. Travelling from Istanbul to Hong Kong/Shanghai and finally returning to London/Scotland, this Bond film is unusual in showing London's vulnerability to terrorist attack and Bond and MI6 battling against the evil genius without any help from their US allies.

The narrative arc also addresses the personal trajectories of Bond, M and the arch-villain Silva. But the film also addresses the role of loyalty and revenge in the covert world of the spy, as well as the capacity of men and women to 'bounce back' from physical and emotional trauma (Dodds 2014). While Bond's resilience is made possible by a combination of luck and support from his boss M, Silva's resilience provokes revulsion from M, even though she abandoned him to Chinese operatives when the UK gave up their hold on Hong Kong in 1997. M's deliberate amnesia ended up provoking Silva to take his revenge on her and MI6.

James Bond producers use and indeed exploit intertextuality in order to maintain audience interest in the film series. Making a Bond movie is big business with filming budgets running over $100 million and a complex series of business transactions with governments, private companies, sponsors and of course the stars themselves. Prior to a Bond film launch, the movie studio undertakes a series of promotional activities, including releasing so-called 'teasers' or 'trailers', which give audiences a glimpse of what is to come in the new Bond film. Bond-related advertising, including product promotion, begins in earnest, and a range of items such as drinks, cars and places becoming enrolled in an intertextual exercise designed to generate audience anticipation and interest. Bond scriptwriters, moreover, understand that Bond fans enjoy and expect those intertextual references, so *Skyfall* (2012) follows the 'rules' by, for example, showing Bond driving the classic Aston Martin DB5 car (which was first seen in *Thunderball* [1965]).

Most dramatically, *Casino Royale* (2006) saw the James Bond franchise reboot the character. Bond, played by a blonde-haired Daniel Craig, provoked initial skepticism because journalists and some fans were unhappy that the new actor to play Bond looked 'different'. In the story, Bond is shown carrying out his first kill and eventually obtaining his revered 'Double O' status. Mindful of a post-9/11 geopolitical environment, danger and insecurity are shown to have a more mobile quality as a new terror-business organisation (Quantum Network) adroitly moves money, terror and influence via cyber-networks and secret partnerships. Unlike other Bond films, *Casino Royale* initiated a serial narrative, and the subsequent films (*Quantum of Solace* [2008] and *Skyfall* [2012]) appear to share some of the qualities of the *Batman* and *Jason Bourne* film series. All three follow a serial narrative, involving a spy or super-hero battling against cunning enemies and, at times, indifferent colleagues. Like Batman, James Bond is an orphan who is embittered by the death of a lover and invested with a renewed sense of purpose to confront those responsible. Reading James Bond intertextually thus would involve us being attentive to a range of intertextual references and contexts – something that is essential when we consider how popular cultural references inform and animate the US-led war on terror.

More broadly, the advantage of thinking and writing intertextually is that we make ourselves more alert to the multiple and complex ways in which issues such as terrorism, diplomacy and war are understood. One fertile area for study might be the intertextuality of presidential and prime-ministerial discourses, and the manner in which key events and processes such as 9/11 and the war on terror are enrolled in what Michel Foucault described as 'regimes of truth' (Foucault 1988). This means that we need to think carefully how even single words like 'crusade' perform a great discursive work by positioning the US and its protagonist Osama Bin Laden and Al-Qaeda in a religious-geopolitical struggle.

Conclusion

This short article cannot do justice to the ways in which popular geopolitics might productively contribute to how, what scholars such as James Der Derian and Michael Shapiro (1989) once noted, the reel and the real co-constitute one another. There are a number of ways in which we might engage with popular media, such as film and television, and the war on terror (for a wider review, see Holloway 2008). And there are many more films, television programmes, video games, toys and novels to mention, but a few that could be productively considered to be part of the popular geopolitics of the war on terror.

There is clearly a broader landscape to consider when it comes to thinking further how everyday lives are enrolled and enmeshed in popular cultural objects and circuits. I have highlighted three ways – representational logics, emotion and affect, and intertextuality. Each provides an approach that offers insights into how popular geopolitics connects to the war on terror – by asking us and others to consider how threats and danger get imagined, how we might feel about security and insecurity, and how we might even take pleasure from seeing superheroes and spies overwhelm those who would harm London, New York and even Gotham City. And finally, how we make sense (constantly) of individuals, events and processes by making reference to other texts and sources, including popular cultural ones.

Acknowledgements

My thanks to Federica Caso and Caitlin Hamilton for the kind invitation to participate in this project, and to Peter Adey for his comments on an earlier draft.

References

Bleiker, R. (2001) 'The aesthetic turn in international political heory', *Millennium: Journal of International Studies*, 30(3): 509-533.

Carter, S. and K. Dodds (2014) *International Politics and Film*, New York: Columbia University Press.

Der Derian, J. (2009) *Virtuous War*, London: Routledge.

Der Derian, J. and M. Shapiro (ed)(1998) *International/Inter-textual Relations: Postmodern Readings of World Politics*, Lexington: Lexington Books.

Dittmer, J. (2005) 'Captain America's Empire: Reflections on identity, popular culture, and post-9/11 geopolitics', *Annals of the Association of American Geographers*, 95(3): 626-643.

Dittmer, J. (2011) 'American exceptionalism, visual effects, and the post-9/11 cinematic superhero boom', *Environment and Planning D: Society and Space*, 29(1): 114-130.

Dodds, K. (2013) '"I'm still not crossing that": Borders, dispossession and sovereignty in Frozen River (2008)', *Geopolitics*, 18(3): 560-583.

Dodds, K. (2014) 'Shaking and stirring James Bond: Age, gender, and resilience in Skyfall (2012)', *Journal of Popular Film and Television*, 42(2).

Dodds, K., M. Kuus and J. Sharp (eds)(2013) *The Ashgate Companion to Critical Geopolitics*, Farnham: Ashgate.

Foucault, M. (1988) *The History of Sexuality: The Will to Knowledge*, London: Penguin.

Holloway, D. (2008) *9/11 and the War on Terror*, Edinburgh: Edinburgh University Press.

Jefford, S. (1994) *Hard Bodies*, Rutgers: Rutgers University Press.

Keane, S. (2006) *Disaster Movies*, London: Wallflower Press.

Massumi, B. (2002) *Parables for the Virtual*, Durham: Duke University Press.

Moore, C. and L. J. Shepherd (2010) 'Aesthetics and International Relations: Towards a global politics', *Global Society*, 24(3): 299-309.

Puar, J. (2007) *Terrorist Assemblages*, Durham: Duke University Press.

Rich, F. (2007) *The Greatest Story Ever Sold: The Decline and Fall of Truth in Bush's America*, Harmondworth: Penguin.

Robb, D. (2004) *Operation Hollywood: How the Pentagon Shapes and Censors Movies*, New York: Prometheus Books.

Shepherd, L. J. (2013) *Gender, Violence and Popular Culture: Telling Stories*, London: Routledge.

Stockwell, S. (2005) 'The manufacture of world order: The security services and the movie industry', *M/C Journal: A Journal of Media and Culture*, 7(1), available at: <http://journal.media-culture.org.au/0501/10-stockwell.php>.

Weber, C. (2006) *Imagining America at War: Morality, Politics and Film*, London: Routledge, 2006.

Weber, C. (2010) *IR Theory*, London: Routledge.

Zalewski, M. (2013) 'Theorising emotion: the affective borders of Homeland', *Critical Studies on Security*, 1(1): 133-135.

The Hidden Politics of Militarization and Pop Culture as Political Communication

LINDA ÅHÄLL
KEELE UNIVERSITY

Today, there is a growing interest in the study of both visual representations and popular cultural artefacts in IR. Convinced that our understandings of global political events are not limited to news reports and policy documents, in my previous work I have mixed 'real' and fictional empirical cases precisely to make the point that both are representations of political events, both include the telling of stories (see Åhäll 2012, 2015). Theoretically, scholars in and beyond IR – such as Roland Barthes, Stuart Hall, Michael Shapiro, Cynthia Weber, Roland Bleiker, Laura Shepherd, Cynthia Enloe and Judith Butler – have encouraged me to expand my horizons, not only on what is considered 'text', but also of what is considered 'politics' to begin with. As Weber eloquently puts it: '*All cultural sites are powerful arenas in which political struggles take place. Culture is not opposed to politics. Culture is political, and politics is cultural*' (Weber 2005, p. 188, emphasis in original). For me, a research project often starts with a puzzle, a political puzzle that I am academically intrigued by, confused about, or sometimes even annoyed with. Then, to 'solve' the puzzle in question, the following quote by Bleiker justifies my ambition to multiply 'the sites and categories that count as political' by 'going cultural' (Weldes 2003, p. 6):

> If a puzzle is the main research challenge, then it can be addressed with all means available, independently of their provenance or label. A source may stem from this or that discipline, it may be academically sanctioned or not, expressed in prose or poetic form, it may be language based on visual or musical or take any other shape or form: it is legitimate as long as it helps to illuminate the puzzle in question (Bleiker 2003, p. 420).

The political puzzle that I am currently concerned with is militarization. There are two aspects to why the concept of militarization makes me feel particularly puzzled; first, it is often used interchangeably with militarism, and second, feminist insights into processes of militarization are still marginalised and/or ignored. In this article, therefore, I sketch out an alternative way of thinking about not only the difference between militarism and militarization but also the relationship between IR and popular culture more broadly. By combining feminist scholarship on militarization with insights from cultural theory, I aim to bring attention to the idea that there is a different logic to militarization than the one commonly acknowledged: militarization is also a process that functions in disguise as 'common sense', through the seemingly apolitical. Consequently, to understand what militarization *does*, we must analyse the political efforts that go into the construction of common sense. As students of global politics, we cannot afford to ignore the cultural politics of the everyday because this is where the effects of political processes such as militarization are normalised. Needless to say, for me, popular culture is a rather broad and diverse set of sites and cultural artefacts, perhaps only united by the fact that they are generally not taken seriously in IR.

My aim in this article is to show how these sites, artefacts, but above all, *ways of communicating*, are political. To this end, I offer a way of thinking about the relationship between militarism and militarization that I think can help justify the use of pop culture in IR research: it concerns ideology and unconscious ideology as different forms of political communication. This is because, while I think it is essential for IR to 'go cultural', I would also like to encourage a move beyond the use of popular culture artefacts as objects for analysis only; we also need to take popular culture seriously as a form of political communication. I conclude by illustrating my argument about the hidden politics of militarization with a brief discussion of a YouTube advertisement by the Swedish aerospace and defence company SAAB promoting their latest fighter jet, Gripen. First, however, we need to unpack the relationship between militarism and militarization.

A Feminist Popular Culture Approach to Militarization

> A militarizing maneuver can look like a dance, not a struggle, even though the dance might be among unequal partners (Enloe 2000, p. 10).

According to the Oxford English Dictionary, 'militarism' is 'The belief that a country should maintain a strong military capability and be prepared to use it aggressively to defend or promote national interests', but also 'a political condition characterised by the predominance of the military in government or administration or a reliance on military force in political or diplomatic matters'. The result for 'militarization', however, is 'the action of making military in character or style'. In this definition, militarism is a noun, whereas militarization is employed as a verb. For the purpose of my argument in this article, it is also important to note that militarism as a 'belief' indicates awareness and a consciousness, whereas the definition of militarization as an action does not say much about how that might happen. Yet, even though militarism is often recognised as a belief and militarization as a process, the concepts are often used interchangeably, which suggests that the relationship between militarism and militarization is understudied.

In *Militarism and International Relations* (2012), the editors, Anna Stravrianakis and Jan Selby, note that the question of the meaning and value of the concept of militarism is far from resolved. In fact, they claim that the topic of militarism has disappeared in IR since the early 1990s. The reason, they suggest, is that the broadening of the concept of security that we have seen in the years since the Cold War has detracted critical attention from the problems of militarism and militarization (2012, p. 11). Militarism, a concept traditionally linked to states' military expenditure and the Cold War's arms race, has since the early 1990s, they argue, been sidelined in IR by academic discourses such as 'failed states', 'new wars' and 'human security': Discussion of militarism has 'fallen out of fashion in IR' (2012, p. 5). Even though the editors acknowledge that feminists 'have kept the discussion on militarism alive' during this time (2012, p. 4), the book regrettably fails to build on the long tradition of feminist scholarship and peace activism that have critically engaged with militarism and militarization as often linked to nationalism and always linked to gender – the social construction of masculinity and femininity – as a critical factor in the construction and perpetuation but also potential reversal of militarism.

Stavrianakis and Selby identify five ways in which militarism (not necessarily militarization) has been defined or conceptualised. The third conception listed is when militarism and also militarization are seen as the equivalent to military build-ups, an approach that is dominant within contemporary peace research and remains focused on (states') quantitative increases in weapons production and imports, military personne and military expenditure. Here, militarism and militarization are measured through various indicators. For example, the Stockholm International Peace Research Institute (SIPRI) famously publishes statistics on states' arms expenditure. Another example is the Bonn International Center for Conversion (BICC), which has published a so-called 'Global Militarization Index',[1] through which they claim that 'worldwide militarization is objectively depicted for the first time'. The Global Militarization Index measures a country's level of militarization by comparing its military spending in relation to its Gross Domestic Product (GDP) and health spending, information compiled from SIPRI, the IMF and the WHO (BICC 2014).

Furthermore, 'militarization' is normally understood rather literally. Making something military in character or style is most often visibly associated with armed forces and readiness to use political violence. For example, a quick Google Images search on 'militarization' almost exclusively results in images that include weapons or military equipment/personnel. A majority of images centre on heavily armed police officers, reflecting recent debates on the excessive use of force by police during protests and civil unrest, such as in the US city of Ferguson. In fact, at the time of writing (November 2014), a Google search on 'militarization' gives the following suggestions: 'of police', 'of police Ferguson', 'of the arctic', and 'of space'. As I expand upon below, these examples of how militarization is used and understood are not necessarily wrong, but in my view they only give a partial understanding of militarization, and they certainly fail to problematise differences between militarism and militarization. That an institution such as the police force is increasingly getting a military character could be the result of a militarizing process, but while these images show the effects of militarization, they do not necessarily tell anything about the process of militarization, nor, in fact, about the ideology of militarism. In contrast, the purpose of this article is to show that there is more to militarization than what is immediately apparent.

This is because, from a feminist perspective, militarism is not merely an ideology/belief/ value system but also a set of social relationships organised around war and preparation

---

[1]   Bonn International Center for Conversion, 'Global Militarization Index', <http://gmi.bicc.de/>.

for war. This insight in turn suggests an understanding and leads to an analysis of militarization as a specific cultural transforming process by which a person or a society gradually comes to imagine military needs and militaristic presumptions to be not only valuable but also normal (Enloe 2000, p. 3). More specifically, a feminist approach to militarization is interested in the gendered aspects of such processes of normalisation, how militarization links to and ultimately manipulates ideas about both femininity and masculinity. Thus, whereas images of an increasingly militarized – as in military-looking – police force and the Global Militarization Index tell us something about a state's preparation for using political violence, domestically or internationally, in relation to actual military capabilities, a feminist perspective offers an analysis of a society's preparation for war and/or the use of force which is not only much broader but also analytically deeper: by exploring how society in general supports the idea of war. This is about people's, rather than state officials' or the government's, preparation for war.

To Enloe, the more militarized an individual or a society is, the more 'normal' military needs and militaristic presumptions become. This is why it is useful to think about militarizing manoeuvres as a dance rather than a struggle, as quoted above. Crucially, this means that processes of militarization do not only take place in the obvious (military) contexts and places, but, in fact, the list of what can be militarized is virtually endless. In my reading, Enloe's influential research on militarism and militarization offers a substantial piece of the political puzzle that is militarization, that is, what the effects of militarization may look like – as sneakers, bananas or beaches – or how it impacts upon women's lives. However, as mentioned above, I am also interested in popular culture as not just an object to study but a way of communicating IR. Thus, in order to analyse the process of militarization, I turn to cultural theorists Roland Barthes and Stuart Hall and their ideas on 'common sense', myth, discourse and ideology.

In the preface to the essay collection *Mythologies*, first published in 1957, Barthes explains how he 'wanted to track down, in the decorative display of *what-goes-without-saying*, the ideological abuse which ... is hidden there' (Barthes 2000a, p. 11, emphasis in original). Cynthia Weber discusses the politics of Barthes' ideas on myth – that which is seen as common sense – through the concept of 'unconscious ideology', which is ideology that is not formally named and that is therefore difficult to identify. It is the common sense foundation of our worldviews that is beyond debate (Weber 2005, p. 5). Weber argues that we use 'unconscious ideologies' to help make sense of our worlds, very often without realising it. And because we do not realise we hold unconscious ideologies or use them to make sense of our worlds, we very rarely interrogate them. We rarely ask difficult questions that might upset their status as 'common sense' (Weber 2005, p. 5). The way in which I use ideology here is therefore not an essentialist understanding of militarism as glorifying war and military institutions, but draws on Stuart Hall's understanding of ideology as systems of representation. Importantly, Hall argues, ideologies do not operate through single ideas but 'in discursive chains, in clusters, in semantic fields, in discursive formations'. Ideological knowledge is therefore the result of specific practices involved in the production of meaning (Hall 1985, pp. 103-104). Barthes suggests that if we can understand how a narrative is seen and consumed as common sense, we can expose underlying hierarchical structures. He refers to the 'narrative situation' as the protocols and 'grammar' according to which the narrative is consumed (Barthes 2000b, p. 287). In this way, militarization can be seen as a particular security practice involved in the creation of ideological knowledge consumed as common sense, whether it is hidden or not.

In my reading, both militarism and militarization have to do with ideology, and both function as *preparation for war*; however, they do so in different ways. I find it useful to think of militarism as a belief in those relationships directly linked to military institutions, soldiering and practices of warfare, whereas I think of militarization as forming part of the not-so-obvious practices, relationships and politics of militarism in 'the everyday'. In other words, I think of militarism as an open, visible and conscious display of militaristic ideology, and militarization as a much more subtle process of the normalisation of a militarised society. Thinking about militarization in this way facilitates an analysis of how a society's military character is entertained and normalised into 'common sense' beyond the obvious 'military characteristics'.

To sum up, militarization is a normalising process to do with preparation for war: the social and cultural preparation for the idea of war, which relies on a gendered logic, takes place in 'the everyday', and is communicated through popular culture. IR should acknowledge popular culture as a form of political communication, and an advertisement by the Swedish defence manufacturer SAAB demonstrates why this is the case.

'We are Gripen pilots'

The seven-minute-long advertisement video posted on YouTube on 10 January 2013 by SAAB AB is titled 'Gripen NG: a new generation is ready. Are you?' For a student of IR, the Gripen fighter jet video is rather resourceful. IR concepts that spring to my mind include deterrence theory, Responsibility to Protect, postcolonial theory and the silencing of others, international law and legal norms, gender, enemy constructions, security dilemmas, and increased beliefs in surveillance as intelligence gathering; others, I am sure, will find even more ways into political IR puzzles. The narrative structure has three 'layers': first, a voice-over narrative tells an overarching story of intent, of why the Gripen fighter jets are needed in a world where 'there's much beauty ... but also violence'; second, the more specific plot is the action-film narrative telling a story about a particular successful mission for the Gripen fighter jets; last, the video also includes a presentation of technological details specific to the Gripen fighter, all reminiscent of how one might select a weapon of choice in a videogame. In this article, there is no scope to analyse the video in great detail. Instead, my aim is to draw attention to two different levels of analysis relevant to my argument: content and context. Most obviously and visibly, this is an advert for a military product, but it is what it communicates more broadly that I think of as useful for shedding some light on processes of militarization. Content-wise, I focus on the voice-over narrative because this is where the purpose of having these kinds of weapons is most obviously communicated. To me, how the purpose is justified offers insights into militarization.

The film starts with a black screen and the sound of crickets. A male voice says:

> Why are we here?
> Because we make a difference.
> There's much beauty here. But also violence.
> Brother has turned against brother and the whole region is about to burst into flames.
> We cannot let that happen.

Then, the video shows the Gripen fighter jets in action. Overlapping with 'action scenes', the voice-over continues:

> Equipped with the most advanced sensors and weapons wings can bear, we struggle to prevent the conflict from spreading further.
> An unarmed country, desired for its strategic value, it would be overrun any day. So we fly, to keep them safe.
> We are Gripen pilots … . We fly.

Similarly to a movie trailer, the title of this 'film' is presented with white text on a black background. Then the mission plot begins. A female pilot on a surveillance mission in a demilitarised zone discovers military troop movement. The voice-over says:

> The area we uphold is vast, but we can stay in the air for hours and nothing escapes our watchful eye.

The camera zooms in on the aeroplane's 'nose' that has a camera, i.e. the plane's eye. After a brief discussion in the control room, a team of Gripen fighter jets (Fourship Kingdom) are tasked with destroying a nearby bridge that the enemy troops are heading towards on their way to the fictional capital, 'Freedom Town'. The officer in charge in the control room acknowledges that the bridge is important 'for the people we are here to help' and that they would need 'top-level clearance' to destroy it. The president of the host-nation, assumed to be an African country, signs a decree to give the Gripen pilots the green light to destroy the bridge.

Then the Gripen fighter jets are engaging the enemy in the air. It starts off on 'friendly' terms, however. The voice-over, probably enacting 'the pilot's voice', as it has a Swedish English accent, says: 'We meet them out here from time to time … . They know we don't fire without warning, so they make us come in close.'

In other words, the Gripen pilots are trusted to follow rules of engagement. Echoing deterrence theory, the voice-over continues: 'They also know we carry Meteor and IRIS-T, so they never engage … . But of course – things change!'

The Gripen fighter pilots are 'forced to' engage the enemy after it is 'considered hostile'. In a slow-motion scene (think the film *The Matrix*), the hostile combat aircraft is destroyed with the term 'Splash one!' In the end the Gripen pilots manage to fulfil their mission to destroy the strategically important bridge. We see the host nation's president wiping his forehead in an imagined sigh of relief. The background screen turns black, the audio returns to nothing but the sound of crickets, as at the beginning of the film, giving the impression that calm has been restored. The voice-over picks up on the question posed at the beginning: 'Why are we here? Because we make a difference … . We are Gripen pilots.'

Illustrating an argument about how the politics of militarization is different from militarism by focusing on an arms-producing company like SAAB might seem odd, as such a company benefits from war financially and the product it sells is used by states' armed forces. It obviously benefits from militarism as in 'the belief that a country should maintain a strong military capability'. However, as mentioned above, what I am interested in are the militarised manoeuvres that have 'travelled' from the obvious military settings into a non-military, seemingly apolitical, context. In other words, in addition to the politics related to the content, it is the fact that this is an advertisement on YouTube that interests me. To me, the Gripen advertisement is an excellent source for illustrating the relationship between militarism and militarization precisely because what is ultimately 'sold' is not actually the product advertised; after all, the target audience of this short film will not be in a position to buy a fighter jet. Without knowing the 'real' – as in the manufacturer's – reason behind the making of this particular video and its being posted as online advertisement, I would argue that what is 'sold' here is the ideology of militarism and the idea of war as a constant feature of our society. Through a focus on purpose ('Why are we here?') the video reproduces not only war and violent conflict as normal 'elsewhere' but also the use of force as the solution to such conflicts, something that is particularly intriguing considering Sweden's pride in their '200 years without war' history. This is how militarization functions as a normalisation process; this is how the idea of war is reproduced as common sense.

Popular Culture as Political Communication

There is no doubt much more to say about Sweden's politics of 'neutrality' and its reliance on an arms industry despite its long history of 'peace', but that would be outside the scope of this article. Here I hope to have shown that the Gripen advertisement is about both militarism and militarization. This source supports the argument that unless we pay attention to what is happening beyond the most visibly militarised context – beyond the display of weaponry, soldiers and armed forces – we will miss an important dimension to the logics of militarization. There is more to militarization than commonly acknowledged. Thinking about militarization as 'unconscious ideology' offers one way in which to explore the hidden politics of the everyday, processes that will be lacking in IR unless the discipline takes seriously the politics of popular culture. Thinking about IR, militarism and ideology on the one hand and popular culture, militarization and unconscious ideology on the other has enabled a focus on popular culture, not just as an object for analysis in IR but as a way in which global politics is communicated and understood. We therefore need to take popular culture seriously as a form of political communication.

References

Åhäll, L. (2012) 'The writing of heroines: Motherhood and female agency in political violence', *Security Dialogue*, 43(4): 287-303.

Åhäll, L. (2015) *Sexing War/Policing Gender: Motherhood, Myth and Women's Political Violence*, London: Routledge.

Barthes, R. (2000a) *Mythologies*, London: Vintage.

Barthes, R. (2000b) *A Roland Barthes Reader,* S. Sontag (ed.), London: Vintage.

Bleiker, R. (2003) 'Learning from art: A reply to Holden's "World literature and world politics"', *Global Society*, 17(4): 415-428.

BICC (2014) 'The Global Militarization Index', <http://gmi.bicc.de> [accessed 19 August 2014].

Enloe, C. (2000) *Maneuvers: The International Politics of Militarizing Women's Lives*, Berkeley: University of California Press.

Hall, S. (1985) 'Signification, representation, ideology: Althusser and the post-structuralist debates', *Critical Studies in Mass Communication*, 2(2): 91-114.

Stavrianakis, A. and Selby, J. (2012) *Militarism and International Relations: Political Economy, Security, Theory*, London: Routledge.

Weber, C. (2005) *International Relations Theory: A Critical Introduction*, London: Routledge.

Weldes, J. (2003) 'Popular culture, science fiction, and world politics: Exploring intertextual relations' in J. Weldes (ed.), *To Seek Out New Worlds: Exploring Links between Science Fiction and World Politics*, New York: Palgrave, 1-27.

Part Two

SOURCES AND METHODS OF POPULAR CULTURE AND WORLD POLITICS

Worlds of Our Making in Science Fiction and International Relations

NICHOLAS J. KIERSEY
OHIO UNIVERSITY
AND
IVER B. NEUMANN
LONDON SCHOOL OF ECONOMICS

Cultural 'Artefacts'

A growing number of scholars are studying the importance of cultural artefacts – popular or otherwise – for the phenomena that make up the core of our discipline (for a range of different approaches, see Weldes 2003; Franklin 2005; Devetak 2006; Nexon & Neumann 2006; and Weber 2013). Following the pioneering efforts of Michael Shapiro (1981, 1988) over the last thirty years, much of this work within IR is premised on the idea that cultural artefacts are immanent to a general social grammar. Popular culture is interesting to IR theorists insofar as it can naturalise or normalise a certain social order by entrenching the expectations of social behaviour upon which dominant ideologies of foreign policy are founded. In this sense, normalisation is a form of power. We agree with Cynthia Weber that the myths and 'unconscious ideologies' of fictional universes serve as silent, sub-textual pillars of the real. Gestures of naturalisation are phenomena of political power, insofar as such power 'works through myths by appearing to take the political out of the ideological' (Weber 2013, p. 7).

Yet it is also the case that artefacts can be invariance-bursting, that is, they can put an end to sameness and challenge aspects of the social world that we might otherwise take for granted. Approaching the question of normalisation from a Marxist perspective, for example, China Miéville argues that the imaginative differences afforded science fiction and even fantasy narratives can be disruptive, too. As he suggests, 'fantasy is a mode that, in constructing an internally coherent but actually impossible totality – constructed on the basis that the impossible is, for this work, true – mimics the absurdity of capitalist modernity' (2002, p. 42). The finer points of debating capitalism aside, the point here is that fictional stories can, and often do, contain scenarios where the protagonists engage in redefinition and transformation of their regime. Disruption occurs when, as consumers of these scenarios, we discover that we can reason by analogy back to the grotesque fantasies of our own world, distancing us from the expectation that things will always necessarily be as they are.

Artefacts and Genre

In order to be relevant to the theorist of International Relations, readings of artefacts have to focus not only on the political order on display in the artefact itself, what we might call the 'in-show' political order (that is, inside the world the artefact attempts to created), but also on in-world political orders. Relations between in-world reality and in-show orders will, among other things, depend on genre. Genre carries with it its own memory. When we attend a rock concert, we have expectations about what kind of political commentary, if any, we will hear. Those expectations will grow out of certain characteristics of the genre. And they will be different from, say, those that envelop our consumption of a stand-up comedy show or those we have when we watch a TV show. Such expectations will be stronger the better we know the genre, so fans will be particularly attuned to them. By the same token, our expectations about genre convention will frame our consumption of a sit-com as substantively different from a space opera like *Battlestar Galactica*, say, or *Star Wars*.

Taking this broad array of artefacts seriously, then, as artefacts proper to the literary genre of science fiction, the question becomes one of how consumer expectations are subject, among other things, to the expectations generated by the conventions of this genre. Following Cultural Studies theorists like Darko Suvin, we recognise that science fiction is 'a literary genre whose necessary and sufficient conditions are the presence and interaction of estrangement and cognition, and whose main formal device is an imaginative framework alternative to the author's empirical environment' (Suvin, cited in Freedman 2000, p. 16). The term 'estrangement' (Rus. *ostranenie*), coined originally a century ago by Russian formalist Shklovsky, is that which gives the text the power, implicitly or explicitly, to give the reader over to a sense of the possibility of another reality. By contrast, 'cognition' refers to that which enables the text to rationally account for the way this alternative reality actually works. It performs this operation by posing explicit differences between the inner workings of its narrative world and those of our own.

As Freedman (2000) stresses, however, operations of estrangement are not in and of themselves all that politically significant. Texts orientated more towards estrangement, such as Tolkien's *Lord of the Rings*, can be read for all intents and purposes as fantasy. Texts that focus more on cognition, on the other hand, tend towards realism at the expense of imaginative difference, thus potentially stretching the limits of the genre too far in the opposite direction. For this reason, as Freedman cautions, the exact parameters of science fiction as a genre are somewhat difficult to nail down. For Freedman, what is essential ultimately is the 'cognition effect', that is, 'the attitude *of the text itself* to the kind of estrangements being performed' (Freedman 2000, 18, emphasis in original). Thus, even though actual science may someday supersede the cognitively rational elements of a particular science fiction text, it should remain a part of the genre because the author originally understood what he or she was writing to have a potential cognitive validity. On this account, a definition of the genre would necessarily exclude *The Lord of the Rings*, but it would feasibly include the more traditional estrangement-centric 'pulp' of Hugo Gernsback's 1929 *Amazing Stories*, of which *Star Wars* would naturally be considered a contemporary exemplar.

For the sake of precision, however, we might want to narrow this definition down a little. By the time Shklovsky came up with the term 'estrangement', the idea that alternative realities were not only part of literature's remit, but one of literature's defining traits, was already firmly ensconced. A romantic such as Coleridge defined poetry in terms of a willing suspension of disbelief. Thomas More's *Utopia* was first published in 1516. Indeed, taking into consideration that older literary traditions are basically part of religious traditions, and noting that religion is a social phenomenon that by definition operates with more than one reality – there is the profane and visible reality, and then there are one or more alternate realities – we would argue that the existence of what Suvin refers to as 'an imaginative framework alternative to the author's empirical environment' is the historical literary rule. It was only with the coming of modernity that the possibility of a wholly disenchanted literature emerged. In light of this, the oft-heard throwaway line that all literature is science fiction cannot be written off without argument.

In order to refute the idea that all literature is science fiction, we would turn to another defining trait of modernity, namely the acceleration of technological innovation. It is, after all, the 'science' in science fiction, understood as technological innovation, that points to its characteristic type of cognition, not the 'fiction'. By Freedman's logic, there is no reason to exclude the more realist mode of making strange (Ger. *Verfremdungseffekt*) of Berthold Brecht's *Mother Courage* and *The Good Person of Szechwan* (Freedman 2000, p. 22). For us, this risks throwing the baby out with the bathwater. Freedman is right to try to relax Suvin's definition, but we are hesitant to include such writings within the genre of science fiction because the topic of science, in the sense of the existence of advanced technology and/or technology differentials, is not on display in these works. Suvin after all, following the philosopher Ernst Bloch, insists on the importance of the so-called 'novum' (1976), i.e. a technological device whose existence and way of functioning is unknown in the reader's universe or, at the very least, in the universe of some of the main characters. With respect to Freedman, then, we would underline that, at least for routine usage, scholars not lose sight of the dimension of estrangement in their understanding of the genre.

IR and Science Fiction

Studies of science fiction in IR have, to date, focused their attention on more traditional examples of science fiction, whether in written or televisual form (see Weldes 2003, 1999; and Buzan 2010). Principally, they have been interested in the extent to which the estrangements of science fiction have performed normalising functions on the cognitive side. That is, they have examined the ways in which the technologised 'new worlds' of science fiction often retain and repeat elements of the world we already live in, and which we can recognise as such. These themes have a long history in literary traditions, for example in the way self-professed surrealist writers claimed to be more realistic in their representations of the world. Weldes avails herself of the term 'intertext', coined by French-Bulgarian social theorist Julia Kristeva in the 1960s, to describe this tendency for energetic crossing back and forth between science fiction texts and our own world. As she notes, 'SF texts repeat and rework generic conventions, and readers bring knowledge of these conventions, their generic expectations, to their consumption and appreciation of any particular text' (Weldes 2003, p. 13). Such repetitions thus bespeak the reflexivity of science fiction and, as such, its potentially constitutive role in world politics, alerting us to the diverse ways in which the 'real' world in which we actually live is itself a produced, textual affair. Importantly, these repetitions are a necessary and vital element in making a work of popular fiction recognisable, and therefore capable of grabbing and sustaining the attention of an audience.

Beyond this, however, to the extent that these generic conventions might be unconsciously held, they can also function as socially powerful 'myths', guiding expectations of what is normal and abnormal in the social world (see Nexon and Neumann 2006). By studying these homologies or elements of redundancy between the fictional and the real, IR theorists thus hope to get a sense of what these shared – and often hidden or, at least, not overtly stated – conventions and expectations are, and what outcomes they may enable or prevent.

IR theorists differ to some extent on the relative 'separateness' of the cultural artefact and the world that produces it. For some, since the artefact is an effect of the social, it is a worthy object of study in and of itself; there is no need to separate in-show and in-world, for they are both part of the same general text (Shapiro 1981, 1988). Nor is there a need to separate between genre, for all genres are part of the same general text (for a critique of such views, see Carter and Dodds 2011). By this token, studying a popular culture artefact is already studying our own in-world reality, for the popular culture artefact springs from the same general grammar as does any other social phenomenon. This structuralist approach, where the cohesion of the world is somehow guaranteed by an underlying latent grammatical structure, is also widespread within Cultural Studies.

For our part, and contra Shapiro, we tend to see these worlds as being quite distinct. Like sundry post-structuralists, we do not believe that there is such a thing as a latent structure that guarantees the unity of our worlds. Indeed, we follow Shakespeare scholar Stephen Greenblatt's (1988) lead in thinking about this process as an exchange of social energies – or a circulation of representations – where the social delivers the raw material out of which cultural artefacts are made, and cultural artefacts in turn rarefy the social. Greenblatt illustrates his key point by investigating circulation on a number of levels. For example, when King Lear was originally staged, Lear's decision to divide his kingdom into three would have created an immediate and shocked response, since contemporaneity was in the throes of similar divisions and unifications following the Tudor wars. On a more quotidian level, costumes would mark certain actors as hailing from certain classes and would be very similar to clothes used by members of the audience, making for a certain sartorial identification. One particularly pithy example of circulation given by Greenblatt concerns how a member of the audience, in response to something that was said by one of the actors, stormed the stage and killed said actor.

While these two approaches differ greatly as to the hows and whys of studying popular culture, they share a starting point in seeing popular culture as a precondition for action. However, our approach has its forerunners within political science, where, following early efforts by Murray Edelman (e.g. 1995), certain scholars see the study of cultural artefacts as a stepping-stone to understanding political outcomes. Popular culture shapes how constituencies understand the world. Since public worldviews are one of the factors constraining what politicians can do and at what cost, the popular cultural artefacts that contribute to shaping them are indirectly important to political outcomes. For example, this seems to be the underlying way of thinking when Lisa Wedeen argues that work on popular culture may 'show how a critical understanding of culture as practices of meaning-making facilitates insights about politics, enabling political scientists to produce sophisticated causal arguments and to treat forms of evidence that, while manifestly political, most political science approaches tend to overlook' (2002, p. 714).

In this regard, we premise our work on a critical tradition stretching from Russian literary historian Mikhail Bakhtin to contemporaries like David Lodge and Julia Kristeva, and begin with the idea that there is an intertext between cultural artefacts and social life. Bakhtin's central example is the carnival, which works as a play without a scene; performance and social life meet, mingle and mix in such a degree that the one may be analysed in terms of the other and vice versa. Note that, far from being considered part of the same structure, Bakhtin (1984) considers cultural artefacts and social life to be different phenomena and reserves his focus for the relations *between* them. Intertexts must therefore be studied in their specificity; it is not satisfactory simply to postulate that there exists some latent structure that secures homology between a certain social world and a certain cultural artefact. Rather than postulating it as an *a priori*, empirical work is needed to demonstrate that such an intertext actually exists, because of this and that precondition, and with this or that effect.

As scholars, then, what we are looking for are specific instances where we might see a circulation of socially constitutive energies between artefacts of science fiction and our own social world. By energies we mean the pent-up social charges created by human interest in, and engagement with, any number of social phenomena that have come to be seen as problematic; but energies do not emerge if something is not seen as a challenge or a problem. For example, in the late 1960s and early 1970s, a plethora of home-grown terrorist acts perpetrated by underground groups such as the Weathermen hit the United States. These events certainly created a spark in police activity, but they did not create much energy, because terrorism on American soil was not considered a public problem. Compare that with the situation post-9/11. Today, the merest rumour of an attack may set off a widely publicised alert system and spark waves of emotional energy. This change can be observed in science fiction culture, too.

Contrast, for example, the original 1970s version of *Battlestar Galactica*, or even the original *Star Wars* series, which did not feature terrorist attacks. If they had, the potential for creating a sensation would have been low, for there were no social energies to spark. By contrast, the reimagined *Battlestar* of 2004 chose to open the show with the portrayal of a series of all-out terrorist attacks. Similarly, the latter two episodes of the recent *Star Wars* 'prequels' (of 2002 and 2005) featured extensive scenes of parliamentary debate and intrigue surrounding the suspension of the Republic's 'Constitution' in the midst of a terror campaign. In this way, the post-9/11 world certainly sported the social energy for there to be an immediate circulation between what we may call in-artefact and in-world realities.

Conclusion

One of the great virtues of science fiction is its ability to pose fictional worlds that, while cognitively coherent on their own unique terms, nevertheless inevitably maintain a link with the experiences we share in our own world. *Star Wars* and *Battlestar Galactica* are certainly part of our world, in the sense that they are artefacts that belong to this world. The ontic quality of our first-hand world, where three-dimensional organic humans interact according to countless more-or-less tightly scripted narratives, makes for an emergent reality that is different from the represented second-order world created in these artefacts. Despite the difference in ontic status, however, second-order science fiction narratives have the potential to model first-order political dilemmas and outcomes, disrupting and redirecting the political hopes and dreams of our own 'real world'. We put 'real world' between inverted commas here in order to underline how, whatever their ontic status, second-order worlds are unquestionably parts of our own reality. But we should be careful when folding these objects of analyses back into the social fabric that produced them. Against the idea that a general grammar warrants studying popular culture on a par with first-order realities, we hold that similarities and dissimilarities have to be specified in as much detail as possible.

References

Bakhtin, M. (1984) *Rabelais and his World*, Bloomington, IN: Indiana University Press.

Buzan, B. (2010) 'America in Space: The International Relations of Star Trek and Battlestar Galactica', *Millennium: Journal of International Studies*, 39(1): 175-180.

Carter, S. and K. Dodds (2011) 'Hollywood and the "War on Terror": Genre-Geopolitics and "Jacksonianism" in The Kingdom', *Environment and Planning D: Society and Space*, 29(1): 98-113.

Devetak, R. (2005) 'The Gothic Scene of International Relations: Ghosts, Monsters, Terror and the Sublime after September 11', *Review of International Studies*, 31(4): 621-643.

Edelman, M. J. (1995) *From Art to Politics: How Artistic Creations Shape Political Conceptions*, Chicago. IL: University of Chicago Press.

Franklin, M. (2005) *International Relations: On Music, Culture and Politics*, London: Palgrave.

Freedman, C. (2000) *Critical Theory and Science Fiction*, Hanover, NH: Wesleyan University Press.

Greenblatt, S. J. (1988) *Shakespearean Negotiations: The Circulation of Social Energy in Renaissance England*, Los Angeles: University of California Press.

Miéville, C. (2002) 'Editorial Introduction', *Historical Materialism*, 10(4): 39-49.

Nexon, D. H. and I. B. Neumann (2006) *Harry Potter and International Relations*, Oxford: Rowman and Littlefield.

Shapiro, M. (1988) *The Politics of Representation: Written Practices in Biography, Photography, and Political Analysis*, Madison, WI: University of Wisconsin Press.

Shapiro, Michael (1981) *Language and Political Understanding: The Politics of Discursive Practices*, New Haven, CT: Yale University Press.

Suvin, D. (1980) *Metamorphoses of Science Fiction*, New Haven, CT: Yale University Press.

Weber, C. (2013) *International Relations Theory: A Critical Introduction*, Oxford: Routledge.

Wedeen, L. (2002) 'Conceptualizing Culture: Possibilities for Political Science', *American Political Science Review*, 96(4): 713-728.

Weldes, J. (2003) 'Popular Culture, Science Fiction, and World Politics: Exploring International Relations' in J. Weldes (ed.) *To Seek Out New Worlds*, New York: Palgrave Macmillan.

Weldes, J. (1999) 'Going Critical: Star Trek, State Action, and Popular Culture', *Millennium* 30(3): 647-667.

Film and World Politics

MICHAEL J. SHAPIRO
UNIVERSITY OF HAWAII

Many assume that films provide a political analysis when they explore the relationship between persons and forces involved in recognised political issues or institutions – for example, film versions of Tom Clancy's Cold War-themed novels such as John McTiernan's *The Hunt for Red October* (1990), a film about a strategic encounter between US and Russian operatives over submarine technology, featuring a CIA analyst (Clancy's often-used character Jack Ryan) and Russian defectors. The approach to film and politics here operates with a different assumption. Its primary focus is on film form rather than content or narrative. The cinematic art, I argue, is political not because its content references familiar political institutions or situations, but because of the way it challenges familiar senses of reality. It does so through its temporal rhythms – the way it composes images, words, and sounds – and through the way it disables viewers ordinary modes of perception, in some cases with an aesthetic of shock that disrupts habitual viewing expectations, and in some cases by restoring what perception tends to evacuate.

While undoubtedly many films supply what Siegfried Kracauer (1960, p. 306) famously referred to as 'corroborative images ... intended to make you believe not see', thereby reinforcing the dominant perspectives operating within the socio-political order, many critically orientated films summon what Gilles Deleuze refers to as a 'seer' (*voyant*), one who must ask herself/himself 'What am I seeing?' In contrast, the less critical 'cinema of action' continually summons for the viewer the question, 'What will happen next?' (Deleuze 1989, p. 272). Crucial to the way film allows thinking critically is what Deleuze famously calls the 'time image'. As I have noted elsewhere:

> The modern cinema has discovered that the "time image" constitutes a way of reading events that is more critical than mere perception. As long as the camera merely followed action, the image of time was indirect, presented as a consequence of motion. But the new "camera consciousness" is no longer defined by the movements it is able to follow. This consciousness, articulated through modern cinema, has become sensitive to a model of time that is more critical than what such a derivative model supplies. Now, even when it is mobile, the camera is no longer content to follow the character's movement. It employs the time image to think about the time and value of the present (Shapiro, 1998).

Rather than beginning with a rehearsal of what is now a vast corpus of film theory and film-as-philosophy, I offer a reading of films that subsumes critical theorising about film and demonstrates how the cinematic art challenges mainstream accounts of geopolitical history. I analyse Alain Resnais's *Hiroshima mon amour* (1959), a film based on Marguerite Duras' screenplay, which thinks critically about the bombing of Hiroshima.

Although it is Resnais' first feature film, it has a documentary feel. Indeed, one way it has been construed is as 'a documentary on Emmanuel Riva' (Domarchi 1959, p. 63), the actress who plays an unnamed French woman having a post-bombing affair with an unnamed Japanese man. Briefly, the film opens with the two lovers in bed. We see body parts whose morphology is indistinct because they are too close and the scene is too cropped to allow the viewers any certainty about what they are seeing. Duras describes the opening:

> As the film opens, two pair of bare shoulders appear little by little. All we see are these shoulders – cut off from the body at the height of the head and hips – in an embrace, and as if drenched with ashes, rain, dew, or sweat, whichever is preferred. The main thing is that we get the feeling that this dew, this perspiration, has been deposited by the atomic 'mushroom' as it moves away and evaporates. It should produce a violent, conflicting feeling of freshness and desire (Mavor, 2012, p. 115).

Among the political implications of the film is the challenge to the US's rendering of the Hiroshima bombing as merely a final act in a war strategy. In contrast with a strategic story in which the bodies of Japanese victims are rendered in an abstract war discourse as 'casualties', the film renders those bodies in two experiential registers: the bombing's effects on relations of intimacy and the specifics of the bombing's inscription on bodies. Bringing the two registers together – the event time of the devastating bombing and the micro-temporality of the rhythms of intimacy – the lovers 'seem to be under a rain of ash', as the skin of the bodies simultaneously registers moments of 'both pleasure and pain' (Mavor, 2012, p. 115).

Challenging various narratives of the Hiroshima bombing that have shaped US collective memory, which usually includes a persistent 'visuality of the atom bomb' (Steele, 2011, p. 1) rendered as a mushroom cloud, the film disturbs any attempt to establish an unambiguous historical temporality. Through the rhythms of its editing, it shifts back and forth between past and present, cutting between subjective time and historical time and thus between memory and history. The film interweaves three narrative strands, the present love affair between a French actress and Japanese resident of Hiroshima, the woman's (Riva's) story about her past love affair with a German soldier, and the background story of the bombing of Hiroshima. It thus creates a transversality between two love stories and the material and social destruction of the city.

Foregrounded is the film's main narrative thread, the love affair between an unnamed French actress from the city of Nevers, referred to as 'Elle', and an unnamed Japanese architect from Hiroshima, referred to as 'Lui'. That narrative plays into a critical disjuncture for, at the outset, as their bodies connect in mutual passion, their conversation is dissensual. The lovers begin their conversation this way:

> He: 'You saw nothing in Hiroshima. Nothing.'
> She: 'I saw everything. Everything.'

The images play into the dissensus as well, for at the same time that their dissensual conversation is taking place, there is a dissensus between what Elle narrates and what the viewer sees. She notes, for example, that by the fifteenth day, a vast profusion of blooming flowers are poking up through the ashes, 'unheard of in flowers before then'. At that moment, however, what is shown is morbidity rather than vitality; damaged, grotesque bodies are on screen, being treated by medical staff. The musical score also underlines the dissensus. Early on, it has a rapid, frenetic pace, which adds to the tension between Elle's statements of what she sees and what is shown. In contrast, during Lui's rebuttals, his remarks are backed by a contrapuntal, single (seemingly woodwind) instrument, which contrasts with the flute and string accompaniment to Elle's insistences.

With such disjunctive juxtapositions and other aspects of film form, *Hiroshima mon amour* establishes a temporal trajectory for what Mr Shizuma, a character in Masuji Ibuse's novel *Black Rain* (1965) about the aftermath of the Hiroshima bombing, refers to as the bombing's "moral damage". The film literally puts flesh on that expression, animating the process of bodily disintegration. At the same time, it tracks processes of witnessing, while producing a diremption between witnessing and knowing. In response to Lui's frequent assertions that she saw nothing, Elle reports the evidence of her eyes: for example, 'I saw the hospital, I'm sure of it ... how could I not have seen it'. However, when stating that she saw what was in the museum in Peace Square 'four times', she introduces uncertainty into that witnessing by evoking the concept of lack; referring to how the museum reconstructs the Hiroshima event, she calls it a 'reconstruction for lack of anything else'.

As Elle's narrative voice proceeds, the film evokes a distrust of fixed images and iconic representations and develops a politics of temporality. As its narration proceeds, an epistemology of the gaze gives way to an epistemology of becoming, as the film articulations sense memory with a grammatical framing of history that reaches toward an uncertain future. That valuing of becoming operates in the interface between narrative and image. During her remarks about seeing and knowing what is in the museum, there is a tracking shot of a mother and children approaching the museum, and further tracking shots explore the outside and inside of the building. What can we make of those cinematic moments? Jean Luc Godard's provocative suggestion is that the aesthetic and moral aspects of the film coincide. In response to a query about whether the film is jarring aesthetically or morally, he says, 'Tracking shots *are* a question of morality' (Godard 1959, p. 62).

Affirming Godard's observation, the film incessantly juxtaposes the memory of the Hiroshima bombing to the movement of bodies involved in war tourism, especially by cutting from tracking shots of the memorial venues in Peace Square to shots of hands caressing skin. What is therefore contrasted is a fixed institutionalised realisation of the bombing (a fetishising of the event in buildings, posters and glass cases) and a dynamic bodily sense memory, as the two lovers caress each other's skin while at the same time verbally questioning their different loci of enunciation and the experiential trajectories that have brought them together. That they represent two different temporal trajectories – the war experience of Elle, who is shamed in her city of Nevers because of an affair with a German soldier, and that of Lui, who has resided in Hiroshima but was not near ground zero during the bombing – is subtly represented by a shot that shows the crossing of their two wristwatches on the night stand of the bed where they are exploring each other's bodies.

To amplify Godard's observation about the morality of tracking shots, we can heed the way other aspects of the film's form articulate a morality. It is through montage, the cutting back and forth between the scenes of devastation and the lovers (cuts between the instantaneous destruction of bodies and the slow rhythms of intimacy), that the film makes its primary moral statements, which are about the disruption of the temporal rhythms of the life world. Among the exemplary cuts that speak to one aspect of that disruption (interventions into ordinary biological time) are these: At the same time that the lovers are engaged in a slow caressing of each other's smooth, unblemished skin, Elle mentions that when the bomb dropped, there were 200,000 dead and 80,000 wounded in nine seconds. And earlier, as the camera tracks the displays in the museum, there is a long take of glass containers with (what Elle's voice-over refers to as) 'human flesh, suspended, as if still alive – it's agony still fresh'. Subsequently we see 'anonymous masses of hair that the women upon waking, would find had fallen out', followed by the badly burned flesh of a man's back. Those references to both instantaneous and rapid morbidity are followed by a scene of the lovers slowly caressing each other's smooth skin. The contrast between the slow indulgence with which healthy skin is appreciated and the suddenly damaged flesh resulting from the bombing is underscored with a display of scorched metal, which Elle describes as looking as vulnerable as flesh.

The discursive and imagistic focus on flesh, along with the foregrounding of an erotic relationship between Elle and Lui (both of whom are married), effectively lends the film a counter Pauline morality. As is well known, Pauline theology juxtaposes the spirit to the flesh. Denigrating the flesh, Saint Paul mentions, among other things, 'fornication, impurity, licentiousness ... drunkenness, carousing' (Galatians 5, pp. 19-21), anything that involves the 'carnal sins', which are associated with a sensual enjoyment involving 'the flesh'. In contrast, Elle virtually celebrates what she calls her 'dubious morals'. In accord with Elle's indulgence in an erotic jouissance, the film suggests that enjoyment of the flesh – of the intimate rhythms of bodily exchange – is what the bombing specifically and the war as a whole have disrupted. In place of the slow, intimate rhythms of life, the war has produced an accelerated decrepitude.

Ultimately, through both its cinematic form and discursive narration, the film suggests that Hiroshima (in contrast to the way it is rendered in abstract policy discourses and treatises on apocalypse) is an atrocity that took the forms of instantaneous destruction, sudden impairment, and then the accelerated decrepitude of bodies. At one point, Elle provides a brief phenomenology of the war's attack on the body. After looking in a mirror, she wistfully exclaims that she was young once. Imre Kertesz's fictional character Georg Koves (a Hungarian Jewish teenager who ends up in concentration camps) offers a more prolix account of the phenomenology of the accelerated decrepitude wrought by that war (with a Duras-like emphasis on smooth skin). While he is in the Buchenwald *lager* Georg says:

> I can safely say there is nothing more painful, nothing more disheartening than to track day after day, to record day after day, yet again how much of one has wasted away. Back home, while paying no great attention to it, I was generally in harmony with my body: I was fond of this bit of machinery, so to say. I recollect reading some exciting novel in our shaded parlor one summer afternoon, the palm of my hand meanwhile caressing with pleasing absentmindedness the golden-downed, pliantly smooth skin of my tautly muscular sunburned thigh. Now that same skin was drooping in loose folds, jaundiced and desiccated ... (Kertesz 2004, p. 165).

Along with the destruction and impairment of physical bodies, *Hiroshima mon amour* dwells on the ethics of memory, which, through Elle's narration, is articulated as a primary aspect of the film's morality. She dwells on the importance of not forgetting Hiroshima – which is as important, she says at one point, as never forgetting either her former love for a German soldier in Nevers (here, the city name has special resonance: implying 'never again') or the current one in Hiroshima (even though that second love bids to efface the memory of the first). In order to cinematically represent the theme of forgetting in the present, and to do it with a Proustian emphasis on sense memory, the film suggests an equivalence between the two objects of forgetting: lovers and historical events. Elle notes that she had been 'under the illusion I would never forget Hiroshima', and she laments her forgetting of her first love, the German soldier:

> I was unfaithful to you tonight with this stranger. I told our story. It was, you see, a story that could be told. For fourteen years I hadn't found ... the taste of an impossible love again since Nevers. Look how I'm forgetting you ... . Look how I've forgotten you.

Resnais' film has recently returned, with an altered significance, in Rosalyn Deutsche's treatment of the film's mobile temporality in her book *Hiroshima After Iraq* (2010). Her focus is on artistic representations that articulate the event of the bombing with a more recent historical episode, the Iraq War. Conceptualising the critical temporality that derives from the grammatical tense that locates the past in the future – the future anterior (the 'will have been') – she analyses the significance of three returns to Hiroshima. For example, reviewing one of them, she points out that Silvia Kolbowski's video, 'After Hiroshima Mon Amour', 'returns to Hiroshima to confront the legacy of the atomic bombing, linking it to the present invasion and occupation of Iraq' (Deutsche, 2010, p.10). Recasting Resnais' *Hiroshima mon amour* with a different temporal pacing and different mode of oral address, and interspersing images from Iraq, Kolbowski creates a heterogeneous temporal association of the two wars, giving both the past and the present different interpretive significance.

To appreciate Kolbowski's achievement, we have to recognise cinema's present historical moment. As Victor Burgin (2005) has pointed out, whereas once the recovery of instances from a remembered film was possible only if the film returned to a theatre near you, the new technologies of video reproduction and streaming make it possible now to recover sequence images that interconnect remembered fragments from former viewing experiences in order to explore and create a critical perspective. Enabled by the new temporality of film viewing to analyse the film–memory relationship, Burgin gives us an example of his own experience, in which there are sequences from two films. In the first, a woman climbs a path toward the camera and the camera adopts a variety of locations to position her in a landscape (from Tsai Ming-liang's film *Vive L'Amour* [1994]). In the second, there's a long shot of a woman entering the frame and, thereafter, as in the first film, Burgin recalls, the camera positions her in the landscape from various locations (Michael Powell and Emeric Pressburger's film *A Canterbury Tale* [1944]). Because the first reminded him of the second, Burgin was able to replay them in order to gauge the significance of the way they constitute an antithesis: town and country, old and new world, East and West (Burgin 2005). In effect, Burgin explicates the temporal structure of a contemporary media situation that has enabled much of my analysis of the politics of film.

To appreciate the implications of such a politics of film for international relations, we can contrast the way film, as a constantly accreting archive, challenges the more static media within which exchanges of recognition among states takes place. For example, the US's Smithsonian exhibition of the Enola Gay, the plane that dropped the bomb on Hiroshima, and the impact of the event, displayed in Hiroshima's Peace Memorial Museum, constitute fixed stories of the Hiroshima event. In contrast to the museum-ification of inter-state exchanges of recognition, film versions of international events are endlessly repeatable, making possible reinterpretations that alter and decentre exchanges of international recognition. In contrast with museums, films function with the civic sphere, where public culture can challenge official culture.

References

Burgin, V. (2005) *The Remembered Film*, London: Reaktion Books.

Deleuze, G. (1989) *Cinema 2: The Time Image*, H. Tomlinson and R. Galeta (trans.), Minneapolis: University of Minnesota Press.

Deutsche, R. (2010) *Hiroshima After Iraq: Three Studies in Art and War,* New York: Columbia University Press.

Domarchi, J. (1959) in 'Hiroshima Notre Amour', *Cahiers du Cinema*, 97: 59-70.

Godard, J. (1959) 'Hiroshima Notre Amour', *Cahiers du Cinema*, 97: 59-70.

Kertesz, I. (2004) *Fatelessness*, New York: Vintage.

Kracauer, S. (1960) *Theory of Film: The Redemption of Physical Reality*, Princeton, NJ: Princeton University Press.

Mavor, C. (2012) *Black and Blue*, Durham, NC: Duke University Press.

Shapiro, M. J. (1998) 'Toward a politics of now-time', *Theory & Event*, 2: 2.

Steele, B. (2011) 'Hiroshima: The strange case of maintaining (US) collective memory', paper delivered at the annual meeting of the International Studies Association.

Videogames and IR: Playing at Method

NICK ROBINSON
UNIVERSITY OF LEEDS

> It has become evident that the way we experience war history is inextricably linked to the forms it has taken on in media representation (Shapiro 2009, p. 16).

Michael J. Shapiro's pertinent insight, made in relation to the study of films about war, has resonance far beyond its original intent, applying not only to non-war films, but also to other forms of popular culture and experiential experience. This article reflects on the importance of videogames for IR, so filling an important gap in the existing literature. It offers a specific focus on questions of method, proceeding in three key steps. First, it sets out the specific challenges for IR scholars in confronting games, containing as they do moving images, sound, narrative and gameplay. Second, this article explores how IR scholars can begin to work with videogames as a medium. In doing so, it engages with specific debates from within games studies centred on the relative importance of narrative (narratology), visual and aural signifiers, and gameplay (ludology). In setting out the implications of these methodological debates for researching video games in IR, it suggests that a holistic perspective that accounts for narratology, visual and aural signifiers, and ludology (see, for example, Shim 2014, p. 9) is the most helpful for IR. Finally, this article concludes by commenting on the ways in which the study of videogames can function alongside Shapiro's recent work on the aesthetic subject, enriching both bodies of work and opening up important insights for IR, most specifically in terms of how games can be used to offer reflection in terms of the 'the world to which they [the aesthetic subject] belong' (Shapiro 2013, p. 11). Overall, this article demonstrates the importance of videogames for contemporary IR, outlines some of the challenges of engaging with videogames, and offers some suggestions as to how to address those challenges.

The Challenge of Videogames: Methods

> Instead of focusing on how games work, I suggest that we turn to what they do – how they inform, change, or otherwise participate in human activity... Such a comparative video game criticism would focus principally on the expressive capacity of games and true to its grounding in the humanities, would seek to understand how videogames reveal what it means to be human (Bogost, 2006, p. 45).

Videogames pose significant challenges for IR scholars. A key question is, of course, 'What is the purpose of the interaction with the game?' Here I assume that the researcher is actively seeking to engage with/play the game. The reflections on methods offered here are not concerned with 'macro-level analysis' of how, for example, politicians debate games, which requires more 'conventional' methods, such as documentary analysis, interviews, etc. (see, for example, Robinson 2012b). Like films, videogames contain moving images, sound and music, alongside narratives and stories. Yet videogames are also meant to be played, and players have the capacity to make choices within the parameters of the game's ruleset.

Videogames also place very particular requirements on players, who have to be sufficiently skilled to complete the game. Thus, to engage with videogames, the researcher requires not only training, as Ian Bogost (2006) puts it, in 'comparative videogame criticism literacy', so reflecting the present critical capacities of popular culture and world politics, but also the ability to actually finish the game. Unlike films or books, which can be intellectually demanding but, in procedural terms, simply require inserting a DVD and pressing play or turning the pages, respectively, if the player/researcher is not sufficiently skilled they will not be able to reach the game's end, posing significant research challenges.

Here I draw on several interrelated themes – most particularly, visual and narrative studies from IR and insights from game studies based on gameplay, visuals and narrative – to begin articulating some insights to enable methodological thinking in relation to videogames and IR.

Encountering the Game in IR

In order to use videogames in IR, the first step is to consider how to engage with games alongside reflection of what to look for when playing. The focus of analysis is contingent on whether the primary focus is on the single-player or online multiplayer element of the game. For this article, comments offered here assume a principal focus on the former.

Best practice involves playing the respective game several times while taking notes and screenshots in order to capture relevant visual signifiers, record the story and narrative, and analyse the structure of the gameplay. The first playthrough is designed to capture the broad meaning and feel of the game, with subsequent playthroughs focused on specific levels/incidents in order to consider the alternative narratives, examine the visual and aural signifiers, and explore the scope of the gameplay options available to the player. Such an approach enables reflection on key questions: What are the choices open to me? How can I complete this objective? Does the game allow alternative patterns of play? In asking such questions, the aim is to reflect on the meaning that comes from the gameplay options encoded into and coded out of the game – 'the possibility space', in Bogost's terms (2007, 2008. For a discussion, see below).

A further challenge posed by games for IR scholars centres on the scale of 'freedom' afforded to the player. The game *Far Cry 4* (2014), while ostensibly a story-based single-player game, demonstrates the issue: the 'freedom' of the game's open world is integral to the player's experience and thus to the game's meaning, prompting players to 'tell their own stories' about their in-game experiences. Such a game poses significant research challenges compared to a relatively linear game such as those in the *Call of Duty* (CoD) series, where the single-player campaign is similar for all players. In CoD, for example, while you can deviate briefly to find collectibles, the game forces a restart if you leave the mission area. The player's primary role throughout the games is to navigate relatively linear 'corridors' and to literally 'follow their (squad) leader', so narrowing the variety of gameplay-based experiences which players can have within the game. Of course, this does not preclude players from being affected in different ways by 'linear games' such as CoD, nor does it mean they will read the same meanings into their experiences. However, it does mean that in a relatively linear game, the researcher can be reasonably certain that what they experience will be similar to that of other players.

Narrative vs. Visuals/Sound vs. Gameplay: Privileging One Over the Others?

The various disciplines that engage with video games – including literary studies, film studies and game studies – raise important questions as to whether or not the analysis should privilege the game's narrative, visual and aural elements, or gameplay, or try to capture them all. This is an issue shared by the IR scholar. Frequently termed the 'narratology vs. ludology debate', it explicitly engages with asking: should we privilege a theory of narrative to explain games or a theory of gameplay? (See Egenfeldt-Nielsen, Smith and Tosca 2013, pp. 213-19, for a review). The central question is what the researcher prioritises in their encounter and engagement with the game. For example, in line with literary theory, is the story/narrative most important? Or, in line with film studies, is what we 'see' and 'hear' most important, and how important is the game's *mise-en-scène*? (King and Krzywinska 2006, pp. 119-21). Or finally, in line with game studies, is gameplay primary? Here, I contend – reflective of the position within most recent games studies scholarship – that for IR scholars to privilege one over the other is counterproductive, because this selective analysis eludes the multi-sensorial and composite experience that video games offer (see, for example, Frasca 2003 on combining literary approaches and gameplay; Murray 1997 and Aarseth 1997 on the interrelationship between narrative and the interpretative requirements posed for the 'reader' [player] by the rules within games). That said, it can be helpful to separate these themes – narrative, visuals and gameplay – to facilitate analysis, and I will offer a brief commentary on each of them in turn to show how scholars have considered these different aspects.

Narrative

Reflective of the growing narrative turn in IR (see, for example, Dauphinée 2013; Edkins 2013; Jackson 2014; Park-Kang 2015), a number of games-studies scholars emphasise the primary importance of narrative. In particular, they argue that narratives are made up of several interrelated elements: 'the chronological order of the events themselves (story), their verbal or visual representation (text), and the act of telling or writing (narration)' (Egenfeldt-Nielsen, Smith and Tosca 2013, p. 196). Furthermore, narrative scholars emphasise the value of literary theory in its emphasis on literary conventions and rules (poetics), meaning (hermeneutics), and its effects (aesthetics) (see Kücklich 2006, pp. 99-109, for a review).

At one level, a focus on narrative and story makes sense as in purely practical terms: they are both easier than gameplay or visuals to capture and replicate, as they can be repeated and reduced to words. At another level, a focus on videogame narrative also allows IR scholars to draw on the existing work from within IR that emphasises narrative, so positioning this approach on firm methodological and theoretical foundations.

Visual

Similarly to the case of narrative, there is also a growing 'visual turn in IR' (e.g. Campbell 2007; Dauphinée 2007; Möller 2007) that differentiates between static and moving images in its focus. As perhaps one of the pre-eminent scholars in terms of visual analysis in IR puts it, in interrogating visual images, the question is not one of understanding the truthfulness of their representations, but instead centres on the 'question of what they do, how they function, and the impact of this operation' (Campbell 2007, p. 379).

The focus within game studies on visual and aural analysis argues that much can be gained from this approach, as games and film (in particular) share many similarities. For example, Geoff King and Tanya Krzywinska (2006, p. 113) argue that games can benefit from the focus offered within film studies on formal analysis (i.e. the organisation of sounds and images on the screen), and that game studies can take advantage of the terms and concepts developed to study visual media, such as 'point-of-view structures, the framing of onscreen action, visual motifs and styles and the use of sound effects and music'.

At one level, as a highly visual and aural media, it makes sense to focus on what is seen and experienced, albeit with the caveat that this can be more difficult to replicate in words than the narrative/story of a game. At another level, a focus on videogame visuals could also draw on the existing work from within IR. For example, in terms of static images, David Shim (2014) offers an extremely perceptive analysis of photographic representations of North Korea and articulates clearly how he engaged with the photographs:

In considering images as parts of a broader set of representations, methodological attention will be paid to the actual content of images, the context and conditions of their production and their relationships with and to accompanying texts and narrations (2014, p. 39. See also Rose 2012 and Hansen 2011).

Gameplay

> Video games have the power to make arguments, to persuade, to express ideas. But they do not do so inevitably. As we evolve our relationship with video games, one of the most important steps we can take is to learn to play them critically, to suss out the meaning they carry, both on and under the surface ... . We need to play video games in order to understand the possibility spaces their rules create, and then to explore those possibility spaces and accept, challenge, or reject them in our daily lives (Bogost 2008, p. 137).

As Bogost (2007, 2008) argues, games allow spaces for the exploration of rules through a process of experimentation ('the possibility space') and can be used as metaphors to explore the rules that underpin society as a whole ('procedurality'), often in ways that are highly critical, yet expressive ('procedural rhetoric'). It is through this combination of possibility and process – reflected in the actual experience of the player – that games attain their persuasive power and become instrumental to social critique and reflective learning. As Mary Flanagan (2009, p. 249) argues:

> Games are frameworks that designers can use to model the complexity of the problems that face the world and to make them easier for the players to comprehend. By creating a simulated environment, the player is able to step away and think critically about those problems.

The implications of such insight for IR can be clearly shown through a brief example taken from mainstream contemporary military shooter games (see Robinson 2012a for a full discussion). As Steven Poole argues, many of these games, relying on a shoot-and-destroy mechanic, promote a highly problematic assumption that complex social and political problems such as the 'war on drugs' can be solved militarily:

> The more naturalistic videogames become in their modes of representation and modelling of real-life phenomena, the more they will find themselves implicated in political questions, and will need to have their ideology interrogated (Poole, 2004).

Conclusion: Videogames and the Aesthetic Subject

Overall, this article argues that a constructive encounter with videogames relies on reflection on narrative, visual and aural elements, and gameplay. It is thus reflective of the framework offered by scholars such as Laura J. Shepherd in her 2013 book *Gender, Violence and Popular Culture*. Here she offers a narrative focus encompassing spoken language (i.e. textual engagement with the script, song lyrics, captions and graphics, etc.), body language (i.e. the physical performance of each character and the framing of the on-screen images and characters), and non-linguistic signifiers (i.e. visual tropes, the built environment, lighting, music, etc.) (Shepherd 2013, pp. 7-11). Her book thus sets out to offer a comprehensive framework and precision in what she is looking at and how she is seeing and hearing when she watches a collection of TV series to demonstrate that 'gender and violence are mutually constitutive of identities, relationships, (world) politics, and each other' (Shepherd 2013, p. x. See also Rowley 2010, pp. 314-18).

Shapiro's work (see, in particular, 2013) argues that using popular culture to explore the scope of the actions undertaken by and denied to actors within those popular cultural settings can allow us to glean important insights into the nature of political reality. Reflecting on the nexus between games and IR, the meaning and insight offered by the player's actions as they traverse the game's narrative and visual arc is given additional importance through his recent work on what he has termed an 'aesthetic subject': 'characters in texts [here games] whose movements and actions (both purposive and non-purposive) map and often alter experiential, politically relevant terrains' (Shapiro 2013, p. xiv). As Shapiro argues, 'their movements and dispositions are less significant in terms of what is revealed about their inner lives *than what they tell us about the world to which they belong*'; such insights have clear implications for the scope of games to inform IR (Shapiro 2013, p. 11, emphasis added).

In reflecting on the value of videogames for IR scholars, many games have rich visuals, stories and narratives that the player experiences through gameplay. Games frequently take 20 or so hours to complete (equivalent to a boxed-set TV series, rather than a film) and hence allow for equivalent levels of engagement and character development. The player has control over the videogame avatar, albeit contingent on the game's 'possibility space' and – as discussed above – their individual ability to play the game. Players can thus tell stories about their in-game experiences. But the encounters of both players and their avatars within the game also allow them to directly experience the in-game rules. The rules which are 'in the game' are crucial to the way in which the aesthetic subject can move through the representational, political and social landscape – there are thus extremely valuable methodological and theoretical insights from this interconnection between story, visuals/sound and rules for IR scholarship.

References

Aarseth, E. (1997) *Cybertext: Perspectives on Ergodic Literature*, Baltimore, MD: John Hopkins University Press.

Bogost, I. (2006) 'Comparative video game criticism', *Games and Culture*, 1(1): 41-6.

Bogost, I. (2007) *Persuasive Games: The Expressive Power of Videogames*, Cambridge, MA: MIT Press.

Bogost, I. (2008) 'The rhetoric of video games', in K. Salen (ed.) *The Ecology of Games: Connecting Youth, Games, and Learning,* Cambridge MA: MIT Press, 117-40.

Campbell, D. (2007) 'Geopolitics and visuality: Sighting the Darfur conflict', *Political Geography*, 26(4): 357-82.

Dauphinée, E. (2007) 'The politics of the body in pain: Reading the ethics of imagery', *Security Dialogue* 38(2): 139-55.

Dauphinée, E. (2013) *The Politics of Exile,* London: Routledge.

Edkins, J. (2013) 'Novel writing in International Relations: Openings for a creative practice', *Security Dialogue*, 44(4): 281-97.

Egenfeldt-Nielsen, S., Smith, J.H. and Tosca, S.P. (2013) *Understanding Videogames: The Essential Introduction*, 2nd edition, London: Routledge.

Flanagan, M. (2009) *Critical Play: Radical Game Design,* Cambridge MA: MIT Press.

Franklin, M. (ed.) (2005) *Resounding International Relations: On Music, Culture, and Politics,* London: Palgrave Macmillan.

Frasca, G. (2003) 'Ludologists love stories, too: notes from a debate that never took place', paper presented to DIGRA conference, Utrecht, <http://www.ludology.org/articles/Frasca_LevelUp2003.pdf> [accessed 7 January 2015].

Hansen, L. (2011) 'Theorizing the image for security studies: Visual securitization and the Muhammad cartoon crisis', *European Journal of International Relations*, 17(1): 51-74.

Jackson, R. (2014) *Confessions of a Terrorist: A Novel,* London: Zed Books.

King, G. and Krzywinska, T. (2006) 'Film studies and digital games', in J. Rutter and J. Bryce (eds) *Understanding Digital Games*, London: Sage, 112-28.

Kücklich, J. (2006) 'Literary theory and digital games' in J. Rutter and J. Bryce (eds) *Understanding Digital Games*, London: Sage, 95-111.

Möller, F. (2007) 'Photographic interventions in post-9/11 security policy', *Security Dialogue*, 38(2): 179-96.

Murray, J. (1997) *Hamlet on the Holodeck: The Future of Narrative in Cyberspace*, Cambridge, MA: MIT Press.

Park-Kang, S. (2015) 'Fictional IR and imagination: Advancing narrative approaches', *Review of International Studies*, early view.

Poole, S. (2004) *Trigger Happy: The Inner Life of Videogames*, revised edition, Afterword. London: Fourth Estate.

Robinson, N. (2012a) 'Videogames, persuasion and the War on Terror: Escaping or embedding the military–entertainment complex?', *Political Studies*, 60(3): 504-22.

Robinson, N. (2012b) 'Videogames and violence: Legislating on the "Politics of Confusion"', *Political Quarterly*, 83(2): 414-23.

Rose, G. (2012) *Visual Methodologies: An Introduction to Researching with Visual Materials,* 3rd edition, London: Sage.

Rowley, C. (2010) 'Popular culture and the politics of the visual', in L.J. Shepherd (ed.) *Gender Matters in Global Politics: A Feminist Introduction to International Relations,* London: Routledge, 309-25.

Shapiro, M.J. (2009) *Cinematic Geopolitics,* Abingdon: Routledge.

Shapiro, M.J. (2013) *Studies in Trans-Disciplinary Method: After the Aesthetic Turn*, London: Routledge.

Shepherd, L.J. (2013) *Gender, Violence and Popular Culture: Telling Stories*, London: Routledge.

Shim, D. (2014) *Visual Politics and North Korea: Seeing is Believing,* London: Routledge.

Military Videogames, Geopolitics and Methods

DANIEL BOS
NEWCASTLE UNIVERSITY

Military-themed videogames continue to catch the interest of scholars in International Relations and Political Geography (Power 2007, Salter 2011, Huntemann and Payne 2010, and see also the healthy debate emerging from E-IR).[1] While research has explored and problematised the militarised, orientalised, masculinised, geopolitical narratives that encapsulate this genre of games, little research has focused on the individuals who actually play them.

Robbie Cooper's art installation 'Immersion' (2008)[2] shows players engaging with the popular military videogame *Call of Duty: Modern Warfare*. The subsequent footage offers an innovative and unique insight into understanding what it is to play war and, as such, 'Immersion' offers a point of departure, providing a fascinating glimpse into players' engagements with videogames. What is interesting about this project is that by recording the faces of individuals as they engage with videogames, Cooper's project brings to the forefront the affective, emotive, experiential and immersive capacity of the medium. While scholars are beginning to highlight the role of the media and popular culture in representing and constituting world politics, little work has begun to unpack how audiences actually come to experience and understand the political content and the everyday significance of entering these geopolitical and militarised virtual worlds.

The aim of this contribution is to advance methodological practices and techniques within International Relations and Political Geography. In doing so, I will outline a need to adopt a perspective which considers players and their everyday interactions with military videogames. Methodological approaches need to go beyond academic readings of popular culture and instead focus on the players themselves. While I do not wish to dismiss critical academic scrutiny of the military-themed videogames, more work needs to acknowledge the millions who engage with these games. This is important as players will experience and interpret playing virtual war in a multiplicity of ways which do not necessarily reflect these academic readings. In other words, further research is needed to unpack how players actually connect these political and militaristic virtual worlds to their everyday life.

Drawing on my thesis research, I will discuss the use of a video ethnography, which allowed me to capture the act of playing military-themed videogames in its situated context. As I will outline, this technique extends analysis beyond the screen and focuses on what players actually do in respect to their embodied engagements of playing war. In doing so, this approach sheds methodological light on the connections between everyday life, popular culture and international relations.

---

[1]　Schulzke, M. (2014) 'Video Games and the Simulation of International Conflict', E-International Relations, <http://www.e-ir.info/2014/08/01/video-games-and-the-simulation-of-international-conflict/>.

[2]　Cooper, R. (2008) 'Immersion (for web site)', YouTube, <https://www.youtube.com/watch?v=ADMeE8U7eYo>.

Turning to the Players

Over the last decade, military first-person-shooter videogames, such as *Call of Duty* and *Battlefield*, have come to dominate the entertainment landscape. As a result, there is a growing body of scholarship that is taking the videogame medium and military genre seriously. As Power (2007, p. 272) notes, the narratives within these games engender 'a growing desire to mirror "real" world conflict scenarios'. But, as we have seen with the recent release of *Call of Duty: Advanced Warfare*, the producers of games increasingly endeavour to imagine futuristic geopolitical power struggles and the military strategies and technologies to overcome them.

While scholars have unpacked the significance of the relationship between videogames and the military, and the particular (geo)political narratives and ideologies that are embedded in these virtual worlds, the players themselves have been overlooked. In this respect, studies fail to consider how players interact with videogames and how they are situated in their everyday life. As a consequence, audiences are often explicitly and implicitly rendered as passive dupes to the content with which they engage. However, as Huntemann (2010) has pointed out, players are not unreflective of the political and militarised worlds they virtually inhabit. Instead, they are capable of critically reflecting on the games, as well as the geopolitical and militarised content. Players do not necessarily share the same interpretations, nor do they necessarily subscribe to the producers' intended meanings. As Grayson, Davies and Philpott (2009, p. 159) suggest, we need to acknowledge that

> Audiences have repeatedly proven themselves capable of highly sophisticated readings of [videogames], films, songs and politics and are therefore difficult to capture in ways intended by producers of cultural and political products.

Furthermore, the relationship between players and producers is increasingly becoming blurred and players are informing videogame content production. In certain instances, criticism and feedback from players, and the media more generally, have forced producers, in some instances, to modify and alter game content.[3] Yet there remains a disappointing lack of research which has explored how these popular mediations of geopolitics and military violence are actually engaged with, consumed and understood.

---

[3] Plunkett, L. (2012) 'Modern Warfare Map Removed After Complaints from Muslim Gamers', Kotaku, <http://kotaku.com/5949764/modern-warfare--map-removed-after-complaints-from-muslim-gamers>.

One field that has begun to explore these issues of audiences in more detail is popular geopolitics. For Dittmer and Dodds (2008, p. 454), examining audiences is important as popular culture 'provides cultural resources from which audiences construct meaning in their lives, and from which they base geopolitical decisions both large and small'. In order to develop the burgeoning interest between world politics and popular culture, we need to expand the scope to incorporate in-depth, grounded, empirical understandings of how popular culture shapes particular political identities and sensibilities.

In addition to this agenda, it is also important to recognise the affective capacity of these virtual worlds. As demonstrated in Robbie Cooper's project, videogames and play operate beyond the discursive, and involve fast, fleeting, visceral moments of high intensity. It illustrates the experiential and embodied aspects of play. This, as I will go on to suggest, expands on 'more-than-representational' approaches, which are gaining interest within Political Geography and IR.

Moving Beyond the Representational

Studies examining the political significance of popular culture have largely been preoccupied with deconstructing their political and cultural representations. This has been to the detriment of acknowledging the role popular culture has in the everyday. To alleviate this tendency to focus on text, scholars have begun to advocate a need to go beyond representation – to examine the everyday, lived practices, or what Thrift (2000) described as the 'little things'. Allied with the emergence of Non-Representational Theory (NRT) in the social sciences, this agenda has sought to expand analysis that foregrounds the multiple relations, happenings and practices that constitute the everyday. This, as Dittmer and Gray (2010) have suggested, paves the way for examinations of the relationships between geopolitics and the everyday, and is responsive to the ways geopolitical sensibilities are constituted in everyday engagements, practices and performances.

So, what does it mean to play war? Turning to military videogames, we need to consider how the militarised virtual worlds work affectively to 'predispose viewers and players to a culture of militarism' (Dittmer 2010, p. 110). As the work of James Ash (2009, 2010) has illustrated, videogames are a highly affective medium that shape and alter the sensory capacity of users. Various technologies and techniques amplify the affective encounter, whether this is through the force-feedback technology of the videogame controller that vibrates in relation to the game's content, the first-person perspective that permits a particular field of vision, or the thrill of engaging and playing competitively with other individuals and groups in online options of the game. Different videogames possess different affective qualities, and we need to consider how military-themed videogames connect to the embodied experiences of players.

In this respect, Shaw and Warf (2010) provide an important starting point for moving beyond the consideration of videogame worlds in representational terms. Rather than focusing on the aesthetical qualities of virtual worlds, they suggest that we consider videogames as affective worlds, 'increasingly "spilling out" of the screen to affect the player in banal, exciting, or unexpected ways' (Shaw and Warf 2010, p. 1335). Gameplay produces a variety of corporeal reactions brought on between the relationship of the player(s) and the screen world. This is not to jettison analysis focused on representation completely, but to understand that 'affects are always qualified by on-screen representations' (Shaw and Warf 2010, p. 1341). We need to further account for the visceral thrill and how players experience and connect with the militarised worlds they engage with. Through discussing the embodied and affective states of playing war, we can begin to unpack everyday relations between bodies, technologies and geopolitics. By providing more situated and orientated accounts, we open up new perspectives that have been continually disregarded in current scholarship. A player-centred approach instead considers the ways militarised and political ideologies are *experienced* within the game. However, this new approach requires new and innovative methods and approaches, in order to capture a fuller understanding of the everyday practices that constitute the happenings and experiential elements of what it is to play war.

Capturing Virtual War

Despite a number of studies emerging concerning audiences, the methods used – including surveys, questionnaires and the analysis of online forum discussions (Dodds 2006) – have been limited in what they reveal. While they do admittedly offer an understanding of verbal afterthoughts concerning the politicised scripting of cultural texts, these methods fail to reveal how popular culture is actually consumed in everyday life. In other words, the attention here is on what audiences say, rather than what audiences actually do. Therefore, we need to consider methods that reveal the everyday, mundane, habitual, embodied and situated practices of playing war.

As part of my own research into players of the *Call of Duty: Modern Warfare* series, I employed a 'videogame interview' approach (see Bos, in preparation) in order to obtain more detailed accounts of player involvement in these virtual worlds. Initially, this involved speaking to players as they played and using the videogame as a prompt to discuss their reflections on the military and geopolitical content. However, this often proved difficult, as players struggled to comment while engaged in the immediacy of play. Furthermore, I attempted to discuss the experiential elements of play with players, yet participants found it hard to verbalise their understandings of the content. As one participant reflected on the military ideological dimension of the games:

It's not like they've got messages in there saying 'join the army' ... [pause] It's really weird playing them. There is a weird feeling there ... [pause] It does tap into something, but I don't know what it is classed as (Peter, 22-year-old student).

As Müller (forthcoming) suggests, rather than overlooking these kinds of comments, the absence of words or the struggle to articulate is indicative of 'the different, more-than-representational registers at work that disrupt the smooth sheen of meaning production'. These hesitations and difficulties in expression forced me to consider an alternative methodological approach that would capture a more 'unadulterated' moment of play in a familiar setting. This involved gaining consent from participants to record moments of play in the domestic setting. A video camera thus provided an opportunity to capture participants' encounters of playing war.

In my research, I used a video camera to record the six participants in their homes. The video camera was set up to record participants in their homes as they engaged in the *Call of Duty: Modern Warfare* series. The video camera and the subsequent recordings presented a number of opportunities to produce grounded and empirically rich insights concerning the everyday relationship between world politics and popular culture.

First, it offered the opportunity to capture the intricacies of playing war. The video camera was able to record the activities of players' interactions with these games. This goes beyond the capacity of other methodological approaches that are more reliant on the researcher's own ability to manually record information by taking notes. However, in adopting such an approach, it is important to also consider the environment and set-up, such as the relationship between the researcher and participant, and the impact the video camera has on the situation. An opportunity was given for participants to discuss their interactions. For instance, the recorded footage was useful in providing a visual recording that was used afterwards as an aid to prompt players to discuss in-game moments and practices in further detail. For example, some of my discussions with research participants reflected on their choice of weapons and how this provided different experiences. Indeed, one participant explained how the weapons and their properties escaped the confines of the screen. Here, particular weapons, due to their sounds and the vibrations of the control pad mimicking the guns' recoil, meant the virtual militarised world became 'embodied, felt, experienced, and lived' (Shaw and Warf 2009, p. 9). Video ethnography thus provides a means of exploring the everyday experiences and the affective relationship forged between player and screen world.

Second, the video camera offers a means of understanding the multiple practices and embodied understandings of playing war. It showed moments of high intensity and embodied practices with players leaning forward with arched backs and dodging virtual bullets. When filming with multiple participants, it also captured the sociality of play and how players worked together and discussed the game and its content *in situ*. For example, the footage illustrated how militarised language found expression in players' situated discussions. In the multiplayer mode, players discussed adopting particular strategies, such as ambushing, or detailed discussions concerning military weapons and technologies and their capabilities. The camera highlighted the embodied and social nature of play and the militarisation that extended into the domestic setting.

Third, it revealed 'the everyday intersection of the human body with places, environments, objects, and discourses linked to geopolitics' (Dittmer and Gray 2010, p. 1673). The act of playing war involves a complex assemblage of materials, technologies and bodies. While offering players the opportunity to virtually immerse themselves in distant locations, the act of play is always grounded and enacted in specific places. The video footage moved the analysis beyond the screen into the realm of the everyday and provides a more nuanced and multifaceted understanding of what it is to play war.

Conclusion

These points just offer a small glimpse into the offerings and possibilities of video-based methods. However, I want to suggest that incorporating video cameras into research provides a detailed and more complex appreciation of what it actually is to engage with popular forms of geopolitics. In this instance, video ethnography can shed further light on the multi-modal and multi-sensual significance of, and connections between, popular culture, the everyday and International Relations.

This short article has explored a new research and methodological approach that draws attention to audiences and accounts for the virtual experience of playing war. Where previous studies have explored the ways military-themed videogames project particular imaginations based on the geopolitical and the performance of state-sponsored violence, a player-based approach begins to unveil the actual experiences of these videogames. The use of a video camera can therefore offer a creative and grounded approach to a fuller understanding of the complex and contingent role popular culture has in shaping imaginations of world politics in everyday life.

References

Ash, J. (2009) 'Emerging spatialities of the screen: video games and the reconfiguration of spatial awareness', *Environment and Planning A*, 41(9): 2105-2124.

Ash, J. (2010) 'Architectures of affect: anticipating and manipulating the event in processes of videogame design and testing', *Environment and Planning D: Society and Space*, 28(4): 653-671.

Bos, D. (forthcoming) 'The Popular Geopolitics of Military-themed Video Games', PhD thesis in preparation, School of Geography, Politics & Sociology, Newcastle University.

Bos, D. (forthcoming) 'Critical methodologies for researching military videogames', in Williams, A., Woodward, R., Jenkings, N. and Rech, M. F. (eds) *Doing Military Research: The Methodological Practices of Investigating the Military.* Ashgate.

Dittmer, J. and Dodds, K. (2008) 'Popular geopolitics past and future: Fandom, identities and audiences', *Geopolitics*, 13(3): 437-457.

Dittmer, J. and Gray, N. (2010) 'Popular Geopolitics 2.0: Towards new methodologies of the everyday', *Geography Compass*, 4(11): 1664-1677.

Dittmer, J. (2010) *Popular Culture, Geopolitics, and Identity,* Plymouth: Rowman & Littlefield Publishers.

Dodds, K. (2006) 'Popular geopolitics and audience dispositions: James Bond and the Internet Movie Database (IMDb)', *Transactions of the Institute of British Geographers*, 31(2), pp. 116-130.

Grayson, K., Davies, M. and Philpott, S. (2009) 'Pop goes IR? Researching the popular culture–world politics continuum', *Politics*, 29(3): 155-163.

Huntemann, N. and Payne, M. T. (2010) *Joystick Soldiers: The Politics of Play in Military Video Games*, London: Routledge.

Huntemann, N. B. (2010) 'Playing with fear: Catharsis and resistance in military-themed video games', in Huntemann, N. B and Payne, T. M (eds) *Joystick Soldiers: The Politics of Play in Military Video Games*, Routledge: New York.

Müller, M. (f2015) 'More-than-representational political geographies', in Agnew, J., Mamadouh, V., Secor, A. and J. Sharp (eds), *The Wiley-Blackwell Companion to Political Geography*, Wiley-Blackwell: Oxford, available at: http://papers.ssrn.com/sol3/papers.cfm?abstract_id=2441326 [accessed on 13 November 2014].

Power, M. (2007) 'Digitized virtuosity: Video war games and post-9/11 cyber-deterrence', *Security Dialogue*, 38 (2): 271-288.

Salter, M. B. (2011) 'The geographical imaginations of video games: Diplomacy, civilization, America's army and Grand Theft Auto IV', *Geopolitics*, 16(2): 359-388.

Shaw, I. G. R. and Warf, B. (2010) 'Worlds of affect: Virtual geographies of video games', *Environment and Planning A*, 41(6): 1332-1343.

Thrift, N. (2000) 'It's the little things', in Atkinson, D. and Dodds, K. (eds) *Geopolitical Traditions: A Century of Geopolitical Thought*, London, Routledge: 380-387.

Collage: An Art-inspired Methodology for Studying Laughter in World Politics

SAARA SÄRMÄ

UNIVERSITY OF TAMPERE

Today, many of us spend a significant part of our days connected to the world via our computers and smart phones, following and/or participating in social media and spending time in various other online spaces. The internet is where we encounter friends and strangers, and it is also where one comes across things belonging to the realm of world politics. Everyday online encounters with world politics consist of various fragments, which are textual and visual. This 'stuff'[1] circulates at an incredible speed from one corner of the world to another. Furthermore, which texts and images one comes by can seem quite random. All of this has implications for what is known of world politics at the level of the everyday. This also may have consequences for academic knowledge producers, since our 'products' – articles, books, blog posts – are just fragments among many other titbits of information competing for attention. I think that if we want our work to be accessible to a wide audience, we need to work with issues and materials that are familiar in the everyday (e.g. various pop culture artefacts) and we need to experiment with modes of expression which could draw in different audiences.

Thus, we should aim to understand the logics of the internet better, if we want to reach broader audiences and contribute to the everyday knowledge(s) of world politics. To this end, I focus here on internet parody images as a source for studying laughter in world politics and an art-inspired methodology – collaging – I have developed for this purpose. The circulation of internet stuff and the seeming randomness of our encounters with such stuff makes it challenging to engage with such material with standard social scientific methods of inquiry. Thus, I have turned to the art world for alternative modes of engaging with world politics.

Collaging is a playful mode of doing research that can be either theoretical, thematic, visual, or all of these at the same time. Theoretical and thematic collaging, and visual aspect as a way of looking at art, can be found in Christine Sylvester's work (e.g. 2009, 2007). Drawing from her work and my earlier artworks, I have developed the visual aspect into a methodology that utilises art-making as part of the research process and presents pieces of visual art as part of the end result (see Särmä 2014). My collages[2] consist of repetition and exaggeration, ironic and humorous juxtapositions, and I tend to use thick layers of bright colours to create texture.

Genre-wise, my artwork generally sits somewhere at the crossroads of Naïve Art and Pop Art, the collages are located more towards the latter tradition. 'Pop is a buzzword. It is cheerful, ironic and critical, quick to respond to the slogans of the mass media, whose stories make history, whose aesthetics shape the paintings and our image of the era, and

---

[1] Stuff is not really a technical or academic term, but I prefer it to more conventional terms, such as data, because it captures the light-heartedness and junkiness of internet 'data' and I think it is a more accessible and less alienating term (see also Shepherd 2013, p. 1).

[2] Särmä, S. (n.d.) Junk Feminism, available online at <http://www.huippumisukka.fi>.

whose clichéd 'models' determine our behaviour' (Osterworld 1991, p. 6). My collages are playful and they respond to questions of knowledge production in the internet era by bringing forth memes and other internet parody images, which anyone can produce and circulate. The notions of what the international is are no longer only mediated to us by mass media, scholarly works, and academic experts. On the contrary, all and any one of us can participate.

In my conceptualisation, visual collaging enables creativity and allows for a humorous and light-hearted approach in selecting and dealing with the research material. Epistemologically, it works as an engagement with fragmented ways of knowing and scrappy research material. Collaging also de-hierarchises the relationship between text and image when it methodologically uses art-making as visual mode of thinking and presenting research. In other words, collaging can invert or considerably shift the 'normal' priority of text over image (see Armstrong 2013, p. 23). Because collaging is visual form it can work as a way of thinking beyond language. Or at least I try to playfully experiment with pushing the boundaries of language-based IR scholarship. De-hierarchialising also refers to the way in which visual collaging can disrupt the relationship between the writer and the reader/viewer as it aims to involve, rather than inform, the latter (see Halberstam 2011, p. 15). Furthermore, visual collaging aims to (re-)politicise the images used as research material and invites the reader/viewer to pay attention, critically, to these kind of images in the everyday.

Everyday World Political Encounters: Internet Parody Images

By paying attention to laughter and internet parody images and wondering what they might have to do with world politics, I have noticed that because everything circulates so fast and memes are born instantaneously, we sometimes come by a parody first and then find out what actually happened. For example, in 2011 there was a meme of 'the pepper spray cop',[3] where an image of a police officer spraying pepper spray was inserted in various classic artworks and other images. I happened to see the meme images before finding out about the incident where the police officer pepper-sprayed protesters at an Occupy movement demonstration at UC Davis. To figure out what had actually happened to prompt the meme, I actively had to do an internet search.

Another great example is the surge of parody images that came about in July 2008 after reports of an Iranian missile test spread in the Western media. Iran was reported to have tested nine missiles, and the news stories were accompanied by an image that showed four missiles taking off. It soon enough became clear that one of the missiles in the image had failed to take off but was photoshopped onto the image, which was then circulated in

---

[3]   'Pepper Spraying Cop', Tumblr, <http://peppersprayingcop.tumblr.com>.

global media (see the images on, for example, the *New York Times* blog 'The Lede').[4] In response to the Iranian photoshop job, various websites published a bunch of parody images incredibly fast. The images mainly made fun of Iran's failures, which were multifaceted. On the one hand, Iran was technologically inept because it could not launch all the missiles; on the other hand, it was not even capable of mastering quite simple technology, such as photo manipulation. Furthermore, Iran failed in global PR and image control by releasing the 'wrong' image to global media (For analysis of these parody images, see Särmä 2014, chapter 6; Särmä 2012). Again, for some casual followers of world politics, the parody images may have remained the sole connection to the event.

What we know about world politics on the everyday level in the internet age is increasingly anecdotal and accidental. The internet is a specific modality of knowledge; it is random and highly fragmented. Hence, our knowledge of many things remains fragmented if we do not actively search for more information. Because humour and laughter play a role in the circulation process (what is shared, how much, how fast), parodies can sometimes remain our sole connection to an event or issue.

The blogs and discussion forums where the images parodying the Iranian photoshopped missile appeared are specific cultural sites, and there are codes/conventions of commenting, linking and giving praise for the best and cleverest images and what seems like a bit of competition for who is first – i.e. fastest – and who is canniest in designing and releasing the images. The competitive nature of parody practices on the internet contributes to these surges of parody images relating to a specific event, like the photoshopped missile incident discussed here. Internet parody images cannot be divorced from real life. On the contrary, even though online happenings and encounters are so often described as separate from those that happen IRL (in real life), they actually, in very tangible ways, constitute our everyday understandings of world politics and our engagements with various issues that we associate with the realm of world politics. In other words, how, in the everyday, we make sense of Iran or North Korea, Kim Jong-il and Kim Jong-un, nuclear weapons and proliferation, is intimately tied to the viewing of, laughing at, and making and/or sharing of the various memes and parodies.

Laughter as a Political Sentiment

Laughter in its multimodal manifestations frames and constitutes the relations of 'us' and 'them'. While there can be no universal definition of what is funny, it is important to pay attention to what we laugh at and how laughter is always tied up with power. Laughter can both invert and sustain power relations. Treating laughter as a political sentiment (see

---

[4]   Nizza, M. and Lyons, P.J. (2008) 'Iranian Image, a Missile Too Many', The New York Times, <http://thelede.blogs.nytimes.com/2008/07/10/in-an-iranian-image-a-missile-too-many/>.

Aaltola 2009) directs attention to power hierarchies among and between political bodies in those moments when we laugh at something/someone.

By paying attention to laughter as a political sentiment, we can see how the various political bodies are located in relation to each other. Political bodies range from individuals to wider social constellations, such as nations, and all the way to the human polity, which is the widest possible political body. Political sentiments, such as laughter or compassion, orientate political bodies towards or away from other political bodies. The more powerful political bodies, hegemons, often make claims in the name of the human polity, or humanity, yet not all humans always count as humans (see Aaltola 2009, pp. 9-12; Douzinas 2007, p. 5; Butler 2009, pp. 76-77). Laughter at certain Others of world politics can violently push them beyond the boundaries of human polity.

Because of the ordering function laughter and humour can have, IR scholars would be well positioned to explore issues pertaining to the humorous. However, because humour and laughter are usually understood to be the lighter and trivial side of the social and the political, the field that takes itself (even too) seriously has not yet paid much attention to the fun. More generally, emotions have only recently made it into wider IR discussions (see, for example, the Forum on Emotions and World Politics in *International Theory* 2014, issue 3). From a social scientific viewpoint, emotions have seemed too intangible and difficult to get at. Furthermore, they do not feature into the prevailing rationalist paradigm (see, for example, Bleiker and Hutchison 2008). The lack of attention to laughter and humour in IR is part of the dismissal of emotions more generally, but it also opens up questions about seriousness in terms of what and who gets taken seriously. As Cythia Enloe (2013, pp. 6, 18) aptly points out, to a gender-smart observer, the politics of seriousness are serious. To default to that which has always been taken seriously in our analysis and topics and modes of study will only serve to reinforce the old power structures.

Western, and more specifically American, pop culture is today globally dominant. Texts, images and references that originate in the West are recirculated and reproduced in funny internet stuff, such as internet parody images and memes. Consequently, the globality that is constituted via memes is a particular globality – a Western one – and viewers and producers are and become acculturated into it (see Brennan forthcoming).

Laughter can be inviting, it can appeal to people to come and join in the fun; 'laughter always implies a kind of secret freemasonry, or even complicity, with other laughers, real or imaginary' (Bergson 2002[1911], p. 12). Laughter can be also seen as dangerous, because it 'is a boundary thrown up around those laughing, those sharing the joke. Its role in demarcating difference, or collectively identifying against an Other, is as bound up to processes of social exclusion as well as inclusion. Indeed, the two are one. Laughing "with" some people usually entails laughing "at" others' (Carty and Musharbash 2008, p. 214). 'Our laughter is always the laughter of a group' (Bergson 2002[1911], p. 12). On the other hand, laughter and humour can be seen to have positive effects precisely because they are inviting and inclusionary and can function as a cohesive force for group formation. They can be important in terms of creating national identities and the 'making of the citizen' (Dodds and Kirby 2013, p. 48).

On a global level, I argue, laughter functions in creating a wider group than just a nation and its citizens. In Western spectacles of laughter at various others, something I call 'hegemonic laughter' appears. It invites others to join in and attempts to create a common sociality, while also demarcating the boundaries of the human polity and excluding some from its sphere. For example, memes and other humorous internet imagery in the case of the nuclear wannabes, as exemplified by the Iranian photoshopped missile incident, incite laughter, which reverberates through various political bodies. In that particular moment, because the parody images and memes recirculate mainly Western pop culture references, they invite the viewer to join in the hegemonic laughter and create a sense of belonging to the West that easily masks itself as the human polity.

Collaging as a Visual Methodology

Making collages as part of a research process is one way of making sense of the somewhat nonsensical and random collection of material. Because the speed of circulation on the internet is incredibly fast, any kind of attempt to collect a set of materials necessarily remains random. Thus, collaging as a methodology creatively engages with the internet as a specific modality of knowledge production. In order to deal with qualitatively different, random and fragmented materials, I have developed an approach that enables the flow of creativity. This art-based collage methodology offers both conceptual and technical means to deal with the fragmentation and randomness. It is impossible to collect a systematic and coherent data set from the internet, because things shift and move. Parodies circulate at incredible speed and sporadically; some disappear altogether after a while for one reason or another.

Furthermore, the visual technique of collage-making emphasises the intuitive parts of sense-making processes. By making collages and presenting them as a part of my work, I have wanted to retain a playful attitude to sense-making and to scholarly work, for both myself and the reader/viewer.

Collaging does several things methodologically:

1. It allows me to use internet parody images in a way that does not only reproduce them as illustrations and objects of analysis of my research, but can also produce the laughter – that is the problematic under examination – in reader/viewer, thus allowing me to extend the research scope from the image itself to the response of the viewer/reader.
2. It works as a mode of thinking that is both aesthetic and conceptual. I make aesthetic judgments when composing collages and this, in turn, emphasises or de-emphasises certain elements that have arisen in my previous analysis. Especially repetition and exaggeration highlight some themes over others in particular pieces of art. On the other hand, it can point me towards new themes and make new connections.
3. Because it is a visual form, it can work as a way of thinking beyond language. Or at least I try to playfully experiment with pushing the boundaries of language-based IR scholarship.
4. It produces pop culture artefacts while studying them. My hope is that the artwork can function as invitation or easy entry point for those not so familiar with academic theorising.

In other words, the collages as pop culture artefacts are not only an aesthetic and conceptual mode of thinking for me-the-researcher during the research process, but it is my hope that the collages serve as vehicles for further thinking for the reader/viewer in perhaps a different way than a solely text-based academic work might. Particular genres think in particular ways, and different discourses make different questions possible (Shapiro 2013, Cohn 1987). Thus, by presenting research as a mix of different modalities – visual and textual – I want to promote thinking as practice of critique rather as Michael Shapiro (2012, p. xv, emphasis in original) describes:

> To *think* (rather than to seek to explain) in this sense is to invent and apply conceptual frames and create juxtapositions that disrupt and/or render historically contingent accepted knowledge practices. It is to compose the discourse, of investigation with critical juxtapositions that unbind what are ordinarily presumed to belong together and thereby challenge institutionalised ways of reproducing and understanding phenomena ... . To *think* rather than reproduce accepted knowledge frames is to create the conditions of possibility for imagining alternative worlds (and thus to be able to recognise the political commitments sequestered in every political imaginary).

For collecting the research material, I have used a method I call 'reverse snowballing'. This means, in practice, that I have done Google image searches with various relevant keywords related to the topic of study or keywords based on my initial analysis. For example, keywords such as Kim Jong-un parody, Iran missile, Iran missile parody, missile envy. I have also collected images by following links from one page to another; quite normal web-surfing, in other words. I have also saved images and links that I have just come across accidentally on social media. What the 'reverse' in the snowballing means is that the metaphorical snowball has rolled towards me, i.e. I have received links and images from my friends, who know my research interests. Through the reverse snowballing method, material keeps on piling up, especially when the topic is one that lives on and shifts and changes.

In the contemporary moment we are constantly surrounded by the visual; as we live in a visual culture, perhaps it is not an overstatement to say that we are constantly bombarded by the visual. We do, indeed, have more and more skills to critically engage with the visual we encounter in the everyday, yet we don't always necessarily notice what it is that we see (see Weber 2008, p. 42). Seeing and looking, or seeing and paying attention, are different modalities of knowing, just as hearing and really listening are; it is the paying attention part that makes images particularly important to scholarship and research. When we don't merely see but look and take note of what we see, we already enter a mode of analysis. Furthermore, the point of paying attention is also to persuade others, in academia and beyond, to pay attention as well (Weber 2008, p. 42). Entering a mode of analysis by paying attention, we can also take note of what we don't see.

Collaging can encourage the viewer and the researcher to pay attention in new, and enjoyable, ways. Collaging does not require one to feel like an Artist in order to pick it up. On the contrary, collaging can be used, for example, in IR classrooms to engage students in something creative in order for them to see things differently. As Brian French (1969, p. 9) encouraged:

> The technical process is within anybody's scope: the materials used are cheap and they are to be found in most households. If collage is defined as the selection, arrangement and adhesion of ready-made materials to a surface, its scope is almost limitless. There is therefore very little to stand between you and the fluent visual interpretation of your thoughts.

We can go to a museum to look at pieces of art as heuristic tool to start thinking about what is missing in IR and what we are missing in our analysis (see Sylvester 2009, p. 181). Or we can gather material and construct collages, alone or in groups and see what possibilities open up for seeing the international, and IR, differently.

References

Aaltola, M. (2009) *Western Spectacle of Governance and the Emergence of Humanitarian World Politics*, New York: Palgrave Macmillan.

Armstrong, C. (2013) 'Ellen Gallagher: Mythopoetics and materials' in *Ellen Gallagher: AxME*, London: Tate Publishing.

Bergson, H. (2002 [1911]) *Laughter: An Essay on the Meaning of the Comic*, The Project Guttenberg Etext, C. Brereton and F. Rothwell (trans.), <http://intersci.ss.uci.ed/wiki/eBooks/Books/Bergson/LaughterBergson.pdf>.

Bleiker, R. and E. Hutchison (2008) 'Fear no more: Emotions and world politics', *Review of International Studies*, 34(S1): 115-135.

Brennan, K. P. J. (2015) 'MemeLife' in M. B. Salter (ed.) *Making Things International I: Circulation*, Minneapolis: University of Minnesota Press.

Carty, J. and Y. Musharbash (2008) 'You've got to be joking: Asserting the analytical value of humour and laughter in contemporary anthropology', *Anthropological Forum*, 18(3): 209-217.

Dodds, K. and P. Kirby (2013) 'It's not a laughing matter: Critical geopolitics, humour and unlaughter', *Geopolitics*, 18(1): 45-59.

Enloe, C. (2013) *Seriously! Investigating Crashes and Crises as if Women Mattered*, Berkeley: University of California Press.

French, B. (1969) *Principles of Collage*, London: Mills & Boon Limited.

Halberstam, J. (2011) *The Queer Art of Failure*, Durham and London: Duke University Press.

Osterworld, T. (1991) *Pop Art*, Köln: Benedikt Taschen.

Särmä, S. (2014) *Junk Feminism and Nuclear Wannabes: Collaging Parodies of Iran and North Korea*, Acta Universitatis Tamperensis 1961, Tampere: Tampere University Press, <http://urn.fi/URN:ISBN:978-951-44-9535-9>.

Särmä, S. (2012) 'Feminist interdisciplinarity and gendered parodies of nuclear Iran' in P. Aalto, V. Harle and S. Moisio (eds), *Global and Regional Problems: Towards an Interdisciplinary Study*, Aldershot: Ashgate.

Shapiro, M. (2013) Seminar and lecture at the University of Helsinki, Helsinki, 21-22 May, 2013.

Shapiro, M. (2012) *Studies in Trans-Disciplinary Method: After the Aesthetic Turn*, New York and London: Routledge.

Shepherd, L. J. (2013) 'Introduction: Critical approaches to security in contemporary global politics' in L. J. Shepherd (ed.), *Critical Approaches to Security: An introduction to theories and methods*, New York and London: Routledge.

Sylvester, C. (2007) 'Whither the International at the End of IR', *Millennium: Journal of International Studies*, 35(3): 551-573.

Sylvester, C. (2009) *Art/Museums: International Relations Where We Least Expect It*, Boulder: Paradigm Publishers.

Weber, S. (2008) 'Visual Images in Research' in J. G. Knowles and A L. Cole (eds) *Handbook of the Arts in Qualitative Research: Perspectives, Methodologies, Examples, and Issues*, Thousand Oaks, CA: Sage Publications, 41-53.

What Does (the Study of) World Politics Sound Like?

MATT DAVIES
NEWCASTLE UNIVERSITY
AND
M.I. FRANKLIN
GOLDSMITHS UNIVERSITY

Introduction

In this article we look at how music can be brought more consciously into the orbit of the current interest in popular culture and world politics. Our aim here is to follow on from an earlier collaborative project in this vein in order to reflect further on the methodological implications for International Relations (IR) scholars interested in incorporating music as an object of study at the popular culture-politics-society nexus.[1] Our reasoning, then and now, is that music and music-making – however construed as art form, creative and sociocultural practice – can enhance a body of work that looks to de-reify received analytical categories of the discipline and thereby continue to enrich its key debates, as diverse champions of critical IR schools of thought have long called for. Music – construed here as an intrinsically acoustic, sonic undertaking and embodied experience – can question predominant understandings that the best way to study world politics is in a primarily literary or visual register, thereby relegating other registers (in this case the aural) to a secondary role.

The interpretative opportunities presented by song lyrics notwithstanding, we would argue that there are many musical genres, indeed many sonic avenues, by which to explore the political dimensions of the 'musico-literary' imaginations that over-determine the modern nation-state signalled by Michael Shapiro (2004). There are new empirical openings, given the many, relatively unexplored possibilities for IR scholars to connect with work being done on the politics of music/musical politics from a sociological, phenomenological and musicological perspective, as signalled by contributors to Franklin (2005), discussed in Brown (2008) and Street (2012), and argued in Gilroy (1993), Goehr (1994), Korsyn (2003) and Thompson and Biddle (2013), for instance.

There are also theoretic-methodological areas to consider at the intersection of research into music-making and the music business, from both an international political economy framework (Halbert 2005, Negus 1999) and practitioner perspective, as alluded to by scholar-practitioners such as Miller (2004, 2008), Mowitt (2002), Said (1992) and Barenboim and Said (2003), for instance. IR scholarship has had to rely, to date, on the work of music specialists in cultural studies, musicologists, sociologists and geographers who have been interested in the interplay between music, society and politics – with or without the impetus of globalisation and its critics.

---

[1] Entitled *Resounding International Relations: On Music, Culture and Politics*, edited by Franklin, (2005) and to which Davies contributed a chapter (Davies 2005), this volume draws on punk, classical opera, examples of 'world music' from sub-Saharan Africa to Southeast Asia, stadium rock, global music marketing, and the Western classical canon. Contributing authors provided insights, and entry points into some of the music, and soundscapes that interpolate, indeed can disrupt the Western, geopolitical and state-centric *ideoscapes* (Appadurai 2002) and cultural teleologies (see Attali 1989) underpinning mainstream Music and IR theory and research.

In this context, our inquiries begin with the insight that even before the web or the rise of sampling and DJ cultures, music has had the double propensity of being a product of a particular time and place and also able to take leave of these parameters; all sorts of music (and musicians) have crossed physical and cultural borders for centuries. Moreover, as music is made and distributed increasingly online and standard notions of music, if not musical practice (composing as well as performing), have been transformed through the influence of electronic and now digital technologies, we can see how critiques of mainstream (read: Western) theory and research in Music and IR have many points in common (Franklin 2005, pp. 5-6). As popular culture enters the study of world politics, taking its place within the cultural/aesthetic turn in the literature, then music has a role to play in these inquiries.

But what, exactly, does a focus on music bring to the study of the culture-world politics nexus on the one hand, of which popular culture is one aspect, and debates about the interrelationship between politics and aesthetics on the other? Both notions remain contested by those who maintain that IR, as an academic discipline, is more social science than humanities; bearing in mind that art and culture are longstanding avenues of inquiry in the latter. Whilst considering music – as both art form and creative practice, integral to how popular culture and everyday life are intertwined – appears straightforward (after all, pop music pervades our daily lives, is a global business, sociocultural phenomenon with political dimensions in various measures), how to engage with music as part of the study of world politics does present some specific conceptual and methodological challenges.

The first challenge is meta-theoretical for the traditional levels of analysis in IR and wider debates about IR as a discipline; namely that techno-economic changes in how music is made, consumed and circulated over the last few decades as a digitised, web-based undertaking underscore the way in which the disciplinary privileging of the 'international' is being confronted by global – translocal or indeed transnational – scales of operations and sets of actors.

The second challenge relates to the way in which micro-levels of analysis are now being considered as constitutive of politics writ large, e.g. practices of everyday life, gender, race and class axes that underpin the way power and privilege contribute to the making and breaking of world orders, political institutions and imaginaries. As noted above, these days music is made (composed, remixed and performed), listened – and danced – to in ways that occur within, as well as across, national borders, filling and linking social and cultural spaces at fibre-optic speeds, in real-time and in time-shifting modes. Audiences and artists who are convening in these multifaceted spaces (online and offline) are doing so as part of an individualised listening or creative experience (through headphones, when composing), at home or on the move, as well as a communal, crowd-based experience; in-the-flesh proximities or on-screen via live link-ups or social networks.

In short, like everyday life and politics, music operates as a global phenomenon as much as it can also be explored as something that is rooted in the local, the parochial, physical boundaries of execution and consumption. The multidimensional and cross-border dimensions to music-making and music consumption, psycho-emotional or communal experience, have become increasingly normalised in computer-saturated and web-infused societies, even as these shifts in venue and means have in turn radically altered the practice and the business of music-making itself. But this, too, is not that new as such, given the longer twentieth-century history of change in the arts through techniques of mechanical reproduction and the rise of mass consumer societies, chronicled and critiqued by early critical theorists (Benjamin 1970 [1936], Horkheimer and Adorno 1972 [1947], Adorno 2002 [1938]).

The possibilities are seemingly endless when it comes to the musical and historical repertoire available to us, as is the research literature and play-lists rich and full of cross-references.[2] The purpose of the discussion below is to isolate some conceptual and practical rubrics for readers interested in taking a musical/musicological approach to well-honed and emerging approaches in IR. First, we offer two examples by way of illustration and as anchors, to highlight the polysemic and multiplex terrain that the study of music offers (the study of) world politics.

We then proceed to look at some of the conceptual parameters of encountering International Relations theory and research through/as music and sound. To do this, we have to consider what music is, what defines it. These questions are what pose methodological challenges to IR, at least insofar as an engagement with them can see music as part of, but not dependent upon, the worldly configurations of sense and sensation, intellectual engagements that also tell us what – and where – politics must be.

We conclude with a recapitulation of our main themes and an invitation for those engaging with world politics as auditory, sonic, and – with that musical phenomena to take on board – the need to be also well informed about how music researchers, along with their colleagues in other disciplines, approach the study of music and/as politics. Scholarly engagements that are also scholarly practice and collaboration can ensure that the work of critical music researchers can contribute to the growing interest in critical studies of world politics and popular culture.

---

[2] For instance, PW Singer and Allan Friedman provide a playlist on the webpage promoting their latest book, *Cybersecurity and Cyberwar* (2014) to help the future purchasers get 'into the vibe of the book and its findings, with the certain lyric that resonated to the realm of cybersecurity and war....'; See <http://www.cybersecuritybook.com/song-playlist/>. See also the CD compilations provided with Miller (2004, 2008).

By Way of Illustration

So let us begin with reference to two recent musico-political events, illustrations of one 'real-life' interrelationship between music and world politics. The first took place in Indonesia. The second was in Russia. What they both share is the ferocious response of local and national authorities, which led, in turn, to much outcry from political leaders and activists around the world, to the music being performed: punk. In December 2011, police in Banda Aceh, the only province in Indonesia governed by Sharia law, arrested over sixty concertgoers attending a punk rock show. While there were no charges made against those who were detained, the police shaved their heads, burned their clothing, and sent them to camps for so-called moral re-education. Indonesia has a thriving punk scene and while conflicts with the police were nothing new to them, many punks were taken aback by the severity and scale of the crackdown in Banda Aceh and its implications for gatherings of punks in both Bali and Jakarta.

Second, a global musical event and political cause célèbre of recent times: the fate of Nadezhda Tolokonnikova and Maria Alyokhina, who served 21 months in prison after a performance of their band Pussy Riot, part of an artist collective that has made its name around the world for high profile anti-government performances in Russia. The gig that cost Tolokonnikova and Alyokhina their liberty took place on 21 February 2012 in Moscow's Russian Orthodox Cathedral of Christ the Saviour, where they performed a 'punk prayer' criticising Vladimir Putin and linking him and the Orthodox Church hierarchy to political corruption.

These two cases, taken separately and together, illustrate the more explicitly political connotations of one particular sort of popular music – punk, in this case – several decades after it first emerged as the music of a youth culture of political – and musical – dissent in the US and UK (Marcus 1990). Punk is political by definition and declamation: quite literally (lyrics are provocative), sonically (loud, three-chord harmonies, musically and socioculturally – as an anti-aesthetic and do-it-yourself approach to making and distributing music (Davies 2005, Dunn 2008). At the time, and since, punk musicians have made a point of upsetting the musical and sociopolitical status quo.

These two events also highlight several contemporary topics in the study of world politics. In the first instance, how the response of religious authorities in Aceh to this concert may or may not support Samuel Huntington's 'Clash of Civilizations' thesis in a post-9/11 context where Islamic fundamentalism is pitted against western secularism (Huntington 1993, Said 2001). Or how the humiliating treatment of the detainees by the Aceh authorities raises questions about states' responsibility to protect the human rights of their citizens under international human rights law. These concerns become even sharper in the Pussy Riot case, as the trial and persecution of these women went viral, led to political interventions by Western governments in the context of Western Europe and US geopolitical tensions with Russia, and arguably set up a chain of events that is still unfolding today.[3]

Whilst the musicological, cultural or sociological dimensions to these two examples have their own interest for other disciplines, IR scholars could reasonably stake claims for having the analytical tools to apprehend the geopolitical significance of such events. In doing so, the music, performances and audience responses become passing references to the main themes of politics writ large. But need this be so? Does this not overlook an opportunity to reconsider how the geopolitics may be just as much a musicological matter? This is our entry point for this article, namely that musically disengaged accounts would overlook how these events and their aftermath cannot be fully explored by separating them from their respective sorts of *music, attendant publics* and *ways of doing things* (Rumens 2012, Davies 2005, Dunn 2008). This is not to suggest that punk music is the only sort of popular music to express discontent and dissent or elicit violent responses from power elites, local governments, social and religious authorities, or state apparatuses (Bennett et al. 1993, Mohaieman 2008).

Jazz, hip-hop and various sorts of classical music have been outlawed, objected to – if not rejected – and directly censored for political as well as cultural reasons (Brown 2005, Wichelen 2005, Ross 2010, pp. 215-259). Moreover, the historical record shows that musicians across the ages have been often prominent political and social commentators, if not activists. The involvements of Joan Baez, Fela Kuti, Bob Geldorf, Bono and Billy Bragg are but some examples of the various sorts of political activism that musicians engage in self-consciously today. Music – like art – and politics do mix. How this mix can make sense for scholars of world politics, and vice versa, is the question occupying all contributors to this collection.

Rationale and Conceptual Notes

In the decade since the publication of *Resounding International Relations*, IR has, in certain ways, opened itself to culture, but it has done so in ways that still remain quite comfortable to the dispositions of IR theory. Indeed, for a good generation now, IR scholars – feminists, Gramscians, Foucauldians, postcolonial theorists, for example – have been

---

[3] The Pussy Riot case has generated its own literature, in some degree due to the strategic and self-consciously global approach that the Pussy Riot members adopted, as high-profile critics of the Putin government; e.g. visibly engaged with an international audience (the name of the group is English, not Russian, and spelled using the Roman and not Cyrillic alphabet); staging the event in the Cathedral of Christ the Saviour and uploading it to YouTube. And persisting, even after their release, when Tolokonnikova and Alyokhina participated in a performance staged in Sochi during the 2014 Winter Olympics. This performance was also suppressed violently, as was witnessed around the world via social media.

uncovering, reconsidering, problematising and beckoning us to the manifold connections and disconnections between the social world and the political. Musically speaking, the most well-rehearsed tune is sung in the key of the international, namely inter-state relations that are apprehended along the classical levels of analysis problem, laid out by Kenneth Waltz (2001 [1954]), embellished and revised since then from within the (neo) realist and liberal pluralist paradigms.

For popular music, pop songs in effect, this entails an interest in locating evidence of geopolitical events – catastrophes like natural disasters or war, social unrest or political protest in the manifest content (i.e. overtly political lyrics or song-titles). Also in classical or traditional musical forms, this focus on political denotations lends itself to an interest in political musical forms (protest songs, martial music, war requiems, for instance), global musical – to wit, media events such as Live Aid/Live 8 with a clear sociopolitical agenda, or excavations of past landmark performances or concerts (such as Woodstock, or indeed the Pussy Riot event above) as geopolitical artefacts. Courtney Brown divides these two sorts of engagement, politics in the music and the politics of music/musical politics, into two methodological camps: representational and associational (2008, pp. 3-4).

We would add a third, one that lends itself to semiotic and post-positivist sensibilities in critical IR literature and new music research: namely the evocative, connotative dimensions to music as sonic and literal meaning-making and political agency. And to that a fourth dimension: embodied affects and experiences of sonic, audible, worlds. That said, we contend – and the literature bears this out on the whole – that IR has remained impervious to the latter two dimensions to political realities and imaginaries.

The converse is not the case, however. For musicologists have shown a steady interest in this intersection, how politics can be read from, and into a musical piece, event, performance or musical output. Or how music-making is also embedded in specific sociocultural practices and political economic geographies, travels across time and space, how it reveals or confronts incumbent power hierarchies of class, race and gender. These themes are also of regular concern to (ethno) musicologists, music scholars and cultural theorists (Bennett et al. 1993, Pasler 2008). These scholars study secular as well as sacred music because music is necessarily a social activity, an undertaking that is not a priori separate from the world at large. And in the history of the modern – Westphalian – state system, historians, philosophers and musicologists have observed if not looked to find the sonic, musical traces of modernity's Zeitgeist and aesthetic imagination.[ ]

To recall our earlier point, the most pressing challenge presented by situating music in IR has to do with incorporating the debates that have engaged philosophers and scholars of music (classical and popular forms, and those from non-western cultures) about music as an object of study and domain of inquiry with its own historiographies, inter and intradisciplinary concerns, and core concepts (Franklin 2005, Weinrobe and Inayatullah 2005, Gilroy 1993, Shapiro 2004). For now we will settle on two working premises. First, that music can be defined as a 'temporal sequence of sounds' (Adorno, in Franklin 2005, p. 10); what sort of sequence, sounds and temporal criteria being moot. Second, that conventional musical analysis can take us quite some way in understanding the core object of analysis.

These key elements by which a piece of music, or musical form, is dissected on its own terms or as they relate to the sociocultural, political and economic context in which it emerges (see Said 1992, Ross 2010, Berger 2007) are variously listed as melody, harmony, rhythm, tone, tempo, dynamics and form; additional elements in this analytical menu include timbre, intensity and duration.

At first sight, these basic elements of music can furnish any IR scholar with the analytical tools to dissect their music of choice, taking these formal elements to meet a discussion of the political circumstances and/or sociocultural effects of the case in hand. To recall, Courtney Brown (2008, pp. 4-5) terms this the associational aspect to explorations of the music-politics intersection. Music that has been associated with a political event or period or a musician who has identified with, or been in turn associated with, politics. Apart from form, and arguably rhythm, all these elements have a sonic component, a material and embodied physics and physiology. And with that, analytical characteristics according to the time and place and historical moment in which the music on hand is being considered, or created.

This is where *form*, and with that the philosophy of music, plays a distinct analytical role; form is at once a conceptual, historiographical and historical discussion, e.g. defining, locating the arrival and then codifying the consolidation of classical symphonic form or three-minute pop song in their respective canons (e.g. Berger 2007). And when we consider those properties, like time or rhythm, that are not strictly construed as sonic, i.e. based on certain arrangements of sounds and tonalities, or pulsations composed and/or compiled, we can hear that these elements also have sociocultural dimensions; e.g. the length and tempi of symphonies from different periods (e.g. early classical or the late romantic period), that of a piece of prog rock versus a punk number.

However, when it comes to theories of musical form, and with this the history of western music in particular, philosophical and conceptual issues remain an ongoing axis for debate – musical form and language treated as a synecdoche for continuities, breaks with the past (Berger 2007) or future portents (Adorno 2002, Ridley 2004, Pasler 2008, p. 49 passim, Miller 2008). Music scholars, composers and performers ponder these connections and disputes as part of their historiographies and empirical (namely music-referenced) repertoires. As such, shifts in musical form, and how to theorise these shifts, bespeak the disciplinary and historiographical demarcations of research into western classical music and then twentieth-century popular music (Brown 2008, Korsyn 2003).

Ethnomusicology aside, and with that the market genre of 'world music' notwithstanding, in the tradition of western music scholarship the rise of 'new music research', feminist music studies and the influence of postmodern thought on the study of the musical (classical) canon have continued to question fundamental assumptions in ways that echo – but do not simply match – comparable ones in IR (Franklin 2005, pp. 11-12, Pasler 2008). So far, scholars of world politics have been mainly engaging with the representational dimension of popular music lyrics (Brown 2008, pp. 4-5) or how music celebrities engage with political processes, or activism, while neglecting the subcultural intersections of particular musical genres.

The punk examples above, as they collide or collude with national or global political dynamics, illustrate why this latter orientation is indeed necessary (Davies 2005), but not in itself sufficient, if music is to take a fuller role in furthering IR inquiries that are of interest to us today.

Musical Categories: Which Music Do We Mean?

The literature on the history of western music in the classical and popular traditions, as well as non-western music, is vast. The dominant narrative in the former case is one in which western music (classical, but also popular traditions) develop alongside the modern nation-state and Westphalian state system (Attali 1994, Gay 2007); a musicologist's teleology that has its own mainstream and critical literatures (for example, Adorno 2002, Benson 2003), as we note above. For our purposes, though, we would like to posit the following conceptual parameters for the sake of argument.

First, we take music as a generalised noun for any number of material and social practices or objects of analysis that are sonic, 'organised', 'found' or sampled sounds of some sort or another that can be created and performed nowadays by any number of instruments, traditional and electronic. Second, we consider that studies of music, broadly defined, can be deployed to consider longstanding questions in the field of IR and can indeed open up new avenues for addressing those elements of social/political/economic relations that are suppressed in international politics.

But we would want to do more, to take up the gauntlet laid down in debates in musical research that took classical musicologists to meet popular culture studies and feminists; practitioners who have been redefining what it means to be a musician and a scholar (Said 1992, Barenboim 2003, Miller 2004); lyricists and rappers who encode the political in allegories, poems and metaphors in their songs, raps and performances. We mean to go even further than searching for explicit political meanings via a musical moment, song title or lyric, to start unpacking the elements of world politics into those reserved for the aforementioned standard musical analysis.

This is a critical consideration of the sound of world politics and of world politics as sounds of a particular order. For where the manifest content as written text, i.e. lyrics, is no longer primary, we need to embrace how sound has physical and emotional properties, as those scholars interested in affect contend (for example, Thrift 2004, Gammon 2008, Bennett 2010; but compare Leys 2011): how bodies emulate and absorb polyrhythms, how the spoken word has also a beat, a melody and a timbre of its own, with a host of cultural, gender and ethnic genealogies to get to grips with (Mohaieman 2002, Mowitt 2002, Henriques 2008).

Third, we will consider music, again with a broad and inclusive notion of what this may mean, as a mobile and motile cultural practice *in the plural* (Certeau 1997). There are different ways of situating music (socially, culturally, geographically) with different implications for distribution of roles: who 'composes' the music, who performs it, who listens and how, etc. Despite these differences, music emerges not in the abstract but in the realisation of a musical event involving the activation of these (plural, diversely organised and distributed) roles and modalities, locales of reception, and sound waves.

There is thus no a priori musical communion of bodies within a pre-given national context; music comes together in soundscapes that are, in turn, embedded in shifting sociocultural, geographical and politicised power relations. In this way, musics connect: articulate and disarticulate multidimensional relationships and experiences, and affiliations that are bound to yet also ignore formalised boundaries such as citizenship, high versus low culture, western tonalities, and cultural conventions.

So, if sound is vision's poor relation, at least in IR, left outside the broad tent of plural but rational and scientific epistemologies that underpin both empirically descriptive and critical, deconstructive analyses, this, too, is a situation embedded in these power relations. Franklin's point on how the study of world politics can also entail ways of 'making audible' sounds and voices not heard (Franklin 2005, pp. 13, 2013) can be understood in relation to the macro- and micro-politics nexus of these connections and networks of social relations.

Learning to listen is not to *escape* from the international (Walker 2010), or indeed the global, but to engage with it. Developing musicological modes alongside those of literary and visual analysis currently in favour, we can render different registers of the political audible. Then it becomes possible to refigure these political registers through, and in musical compositions and creations, performances that include mixing, improvisations or aurally connected bodies that are also physically connecting, even across different physical spaces through information and communication technologies, or acoustically in situ or while on the move.

Investigating ways of hearing, or musicking (Small 1998), the international as but one dimension to the study of world politics today does not, however, provide any cosy guarantees of a transcendental alternative. So the fourth challenge then is how to take the analytical tools of musical analysis, along with studies of attendant publics and ways of doing things, right into the heart of the latest phase of the (popular) 'cultural turn' in IR. This means learning how to unpack these elements; across conventional orderings of time and space and conventional levels of analysis that would put the local and the translocal somewhere far below the higher import of the international and global arenas of political action. This is how we can even engage more productively in discussions of why Beethoven's setting of the *Ode to Joy* in the last movement of his Ninth Symphony (D minor, Op. 125, a.k.a. 'the Choral', 1824) is repeatedly played at major moments of political symbolism, comparing perhaps different interpretations of this well-worn and perhaps symphonic sample.[4]

What Does the Study of Music Offer Scholars of World Politics?

In this section, we discuss three ways of considering how IR scholars can broach music as a field, and object of inquiry, within the current (popular) cultural turn: music cultures and/ as content, music and the senses, and music and/as sound.

---

[4] References to the political and cultural context of Beethoven's time and how his music has been used for a variety of effects, political programmes and associations - e.g. as the soundtrack to political events (the reunification of Germany in 1990 and subsequent commemorations) or cinema classics (such as Stanley Kubrick's *A Clockwork Orange*) – following his death are myriad. Suffice it to say that Beethoven's personal life and political affiliations have provided much material for conjecture as well as for ways into the analysis of his contribution to musical form, and content – the musical language – of his work (Pasler 2008, pp. 28-29, Said 2006, pp. 7-14, Attali 1989). How his music, and that of other German composers, has been (mis-)used for political purposes in the last century is another thread, explored in Ross's chapter, 'Death Fugue: Music in Hitler's Germany' in *The Rest is Noise* (2010, p. 333 passim). And the influence of different performances of well-known pieces, such as the Fifth Symphony or the Ode to Joy from the Ninth Symphony, under different conductors (e.g. Herbert von Karajan, Daniel Barenboim) and their respective political and cultural references (Barenboim 2003, Service 2014) is another line of inquiry; all this without mentioning popular and electronic workings of the same composer; the electronic synthesizer version of the Ode to Joy, arranged by Walter/Wendy Carlos (1971, Warner Bros. Records - K 16145) in *A Clockwork Orange* is a case in point.

1) *Musical Cultures and/as Content*

Along with studies of the political associations that a particular music, or musician, may or may not have are those that focus on the representational dimensions, as Brown notes (2008, p. 5). And this is where most work on politics and music lends itself to IR scholars from an interpretative bent, that is, taking song lyrics as manifest political content even when not explicitly presented as political as such. To want to move interest in music and world politics past the literary– the message-bearing role of the words – in order to consider how the music itself also bears or produces meaning is not to dismiss the constitutive role that words do play. Indeed, some lyrics are explicit in their political intent by reference, if not linked to a politicising moment: anti-war and other sorts of protest songs, for instance. Where the words lend themselves to social science models that look to match political content – and portent – to historical context, researchers can go some way in empirically verifying links between that music and those politics. And in those cases where the political as content is not immediately deciperable in literal terms, the deployment of linguistic methods to unlock the connotations, allegories or 'poetics' (Krims 2000) of these lyrics offers another way into understanding what a song is about.

Words do matter in this respect. However, in methodological terms, staying only with the words returns us to the literary interpretative exercise where meaning is extracted from manifest or latent content, the musical elements and settings for those words remaining moot. But much music, in western and non-western traditions, is without words. Moreover, rap and traditions see words as both content and rhythm and melody; literary – and overly literal – interventions can take us so far that they miss the musico-political point (Miller 2008).[5]

Another musically productive approach might come from taking the root of the notion of musical *cultures* seriously at the intersection of classical and popular music – and cultural – studies, sociology and anthropology. These disciplines take culture as mobile and motile, as an active component of the contemporary world and the historical narratives underpinning it; culture as cultivation and education and everyday practice. Music, in this key, can be construed also as

---

[5] Literal takes on the meaning of musical lyrics, in the blues, for instance, where allegory and euphemism are prevalent, or a lack of knowledge of how urban African-American idioms are integral to the layers of meaning and cross-references that characterise rap and hip-hop texts can infer a lack of political substance or relevance even when in fact the piece in question is suffused in (national and global) politics; e.g. Billie Holliday's iconic cover of Abel Meeropol's song 'Strange Fruit' (1937) is one example where a literal reading of the lyrics would completely miss the political point of reference, and of protest.

political and economic *practices*, which are inevitably, albeit asynchronously, imbued with the sociocultural geographies of *musical* ones. Politics, culture, and music examined as dynamic processes, everyday practices; 'musickings' in other words ... [M]usic and politics are to be taken as verbs (*doing* words, mobile meanings) rather than nouns (naming words, static categories) (Franklin 2005, pp. 5-6; see also Small 1998).

Manifold opportunities for the aesthetic-cum-cultural turn in IR present themselves by taking both conventional and new musical analysis on board in more concerted ways. In this way, even the traditions of so-called parsimonious models of the study of international behaviour can be rendered with musical nuance. Musical subcultures and the political responses they incur – as in the examples of the punks of Indonesia or of Pussy Riot – invite anthropologically or ethnographically rich descriptions of the class, gendered, racial, geopolitical and other determinations of other internationals and their situation with regard to the ethnocentric and gendered biases of the discipline's received wisdoms.

Musical analysis can also produce new sorts of situated, embodied knowledge of the audible politics of everyday life, i.e. hear the 'audible world' (Attali 1994) in ways that need not reduce cultural artefact, practice or sonority to the master historical narrative of modernity and its Postmodern Other. Contemporary musical practices from digital sampling and its precursors in avant-garde music indicate different methods for deconstructing, re-mixing and circulating the inter/national and other political modalities.

This polysemic model for musico-political analysis also suggests the limits of the 'creative genius' (whose great work must be reproduced faithfully) account of music and its isomorphic relation to the technocratic reserve of politics for specialists in policy and diplomacy. Non-western musical forms – and politics – can be understood and taken up as formative of the inter/national and other formations, and not merely products to be appropriated or mimicked.

2) Music and the Senses: Bodies

Nonetheless, culture is no longer a marginal or even controversial area of interest for IR. The literary and visual turn in the study of world politics, and conversely a burgeoning interest in how arts and culture are permeated by political concerns, have brought us far. IR's preference remains for a visualised literary re-imagining of core objects of analysis and themes, for their defenders as well as critics looking to address the imbalance of established western political-cultural narratives. But what about those other senses of perception: hearing and its sociocultural and political economic object of attention, noise-sound-music?

The relative under-theorisation of the sonically embodied qualities of material cultures, of the sound systems (Henriques 2008, 2010) of soundscapes and the massive popularity of non-western, so-called world music that has moved into – or been taken into – the western political and media power centres is anything but a soundless phenomenon. The manner in which the sense of sight came to take priority over other sensory experience has had consequences for how we know things and how we assess that knowledge; this holds true for IR as it does for other parts of the western, modernist episteme based on generating knowledge about societies that are predominately experienced and apprehended in visual terms (Franklin 2005, pp. 8-9); the interrelationship between perception and conception where the (mind's) eye is the predominant organ for observation and contemplation.

Music, like dance, is an art form and set of practices that is non-visual by definition. The main elements of music are sonic, and with that linked to our bodies as receptors and conveyers of the rhythmic properties alone. Like dance, we make and receive music through our bodies, whatever the instrument, with manifest consequences for international relations (Cusick 2006).

In particular, the conditions that occasioned the predominance of sight *disembodied* knowledge. In *Techniques of the Observer*, Jonathan Crary (1992) recounts the invention of the camera obscura. The chamber was fitted with a pinhole, and later with a lens, that projected light from outside onto an interior wall, producing an image of the external environment. The point at which the observation is produced – the pinhole – was no longer attached to the body.

Crary shows how the camera obscura articulated an abstract, disembodied point of observation that in turn created an ideal, disembodied subjectivity that could be assessed in terms of how adequately it receives and reflects a given, fixed, external, objective, visual world. The camera obscura thus enabled the disembodying of observation. Narrative (stories, novels, plots, etc.) similarly obtains a 'life of its own' and appears as a positive object that can be more or less well described and inserted into an abstract international political analysis as evidence or case – this is Drezner's method for reading the Zombie trope (2015). This externalising and fixing of visual or narrative evidence also renders them instrumental, ripe for 'problem solving' (Cox 1981).

Hearing, in contrast, is taken to be a subordinate sense and, as such, its neglect or exclusion from approaches to world politics that seek objectivity and rigour is unsurprising. Where the visual can now be rendered as fixed, external and objective, musical sounds are more difficult to pin down for empirically verifiable observations, even when rendered through critical, interpretive schools of IR thought or behaviouralist studies based on neurological models of how music affects the human body and psyche. This arises because, at this disciplinary crossroads (see Pasler 2008, for instance), the analyst is dealing with a different sort of material; with physical and emotional aspects to the experiential, phenomenological qualities of sound-waves, their reception, replication and then amplification towards and within the body, individual and group (Henriques 2010, Mowitt 2002).

Whereas the techniques and technologies of observation produced a disembodied ideal observer, against which all actual observations could be measured, the perception and organisation of sound as an embodied experience, with physical properties (Goldsmiths 2012) and normative associations (Brown 2008), needs to be taken more into account. Political backlashes against new music, musical countercultures and innovations to the canon are also responses to unfamiliar sounds, coded as dissonant, socially unacceptable, politically reprehensible; the two events in Indonesia and Russia above are cases in point.

3) Music and/as Sound

There is a thriving research endeavour to archive the sounds of our world, urban or rural, human-made or from nature.[6] Sounds as part of our ecosystem and surroundings collected as integral to the audible world in which we live can be heard, and used for music-making; indeed, the mid-twentieth-century avant-garde tradition of modern music, referred to by DJ cultures and electronic composers today (Miller 2007, Lethem 2008), have become non-composed elements of music in their own right. Singly, in sequence or as electronic, digitalised mixes sounds as *scapes*, to borrow from Appadurai (2002, see also Miller 2008), of a particular sort comprise both the sound waves travelling through a medium (air, water, the internet) and the distribution of bodies (sentient, mechanical, reverberating) that produce, receive, respond to and regenerate the audible world as they do so; for some ecstasy, for others cacophony.

Sound is thus irreducibly both a given – a physical and an experiential practise – and a constructed social relation. The *musicking* part of any soundscape produces the affective connections between sounding – and, perforce, dancing – bodies and listening audiences. Music, as something that bodies do in these soundscapes, makes manifest, materially, the connections that theories of affect look to locate and explore. These material connections between resonating and re-sounding bodies in time are what Henri Lefebvre describes in *Rhythmanalysis* (2004): a political *auto-gestion* (self-generating, self-expressing) of communities that may or may not express the identities of territorially locked national states alleged to be primary by International Relations theory and practice.

---

[6]   See, for example, the Chicago-based *World Listening Project* at <http://www.worldlisteningproject. org/>.

Likewise for western music theory and research. As Paul D. Miller (a.k.a. DJ Spooky the Subliminal Kid) points out, fully aware of the western literary and musical avant-gardist canons from which he is drawing:

> sound and the forms we inhabit are intimately intertwined. What happens when you reverse engineer the process, and think of sound [and implicitly music] as nothing but thawed architecture? The moment between sounds, the moment between thought and perceptions – it's one of those intangible structures that give meaning to the things it separates ... that's something to give one – pause. (Miller 2008, p.17)

Miller draws a line here from Jacques Attali and his study of western classical music and the rise of the modern nation-state (1994, see also Berger 2007) to bring both adept and novice up to date with music-making in digital, sound-mixed and web-infused settings. Any exploration of the music-culture-politics nexus has to take on board the formative roles of digital techniques, club cultures and their DJ maestri, and the internet in changing the terms and conditions under which music is conceived, performed and consumed. Via the electric and computer-mediated synapses of an audible world, there is also a digitally sampled and relayed one. So despite the last point made in the section above about working, rather than fine-tuned, definitions, some further conceptual questions are in order.

Like philosophers of music before us, one initial step is to ask (though not necessarily to answer), what is *music*, as opposed to sound – or indeed noise – today (Goldsmith 2012)? Is it an artefact? Is it performance? Is an abstract definition, such as 'organised sound', sufficient, and if so, what counts as organisation? From here, the question of 'what does *the study of* world politics sound like?' becomes a chance to refigure debates about the timeline of the international and its morphing in and out of the local-global nexus through these social relations made politically audible.

In other words, the resonating, shifting, borrowing, disarticulating individual and collective bodies of music are always already potentially political, though not necessarily in the ways and places IR expects them to be. Against the objective fixing of passive and objective bodies that are more-or-less adequate to the qualities prescribed for them, as seen by IR, these musical international relations disrupt the sensibility (Rancière 2009, 2013) that always locates politics someplace else.

In this spirit of disciplinary, sonic sound-systems and unplugged, analogue and digitally (re) sampled crossovers, we would note the need for new vocabularies, analytical idioms and terms of reference. In this case, not from the literary greats but from the musical greats and not-so-greats – for after all, success and greatness have both been shown to be a product of (global) market forces and the mass production economies of scale of the twentieth-century culture industry and its grip on copyright; one that has been slipping but is still hanging on for dear life (Lethem 2008).

The point here is how to move from examining the written text, and hence sub-text, of world politics in song lyrics to examining its integral musical elements, its sonic forms, i.e. how to examine the fact that 'politics – International Relations – can be construed as *audible*; studies and experiences as sound – music, noise, silence ... based on the premise that the "political", the "economic", the "sociocultural" constitute soundscapes as well as landscapes' (Franklin 2005, pp. 7-8).

Let us now turn to the wider methodological implications of the above claims as they pertain to the IR canon and its critics, but also to the ways in which music and cultural studies scholars have broached political questions in turn. In both cases, disciplinarity, in the singular and the plural, is called to account to consider how there is more at stake than 'simply deploying the tools and methods of other fields (the standard version of "interdisciplinarity") but by ... using music as a critical tool to analyse contemporary critical cultural, historical, and cultural issues whose importance cuts across fields' (Lewis 2008, pp. vii-viii).

Wider Methodological Implications

Music critic for *The New Yorker* and advocate for dissolving the classical-popular music divide, Alex Ross cuts right across disciplinary and genre-based boundaries that posit an a priori value hierarchy between high and low culture (in this case between classical and popular music), unprofitable avant-gardist and commercially successful cultural forms that have sustained culturally and economically reductionist defences – and critiques – in the established order of things. He notes that:

> [Writing] about music isn't especially difficult ... [We need] to demystify the art to some extent, dispel the hocus-pocus, while still respecting the boundless human complexity that gives it life (Ross 2011, pp. xiii-xiv).

Ross' observation above resonates with the methodologically and conceptually polyglot spirit that has been at the heart of a boom in studies of popular culture in Politics and International Relations departments across the UK, Western Europe and the US. Can an engagement with a more inclusive conception of music similarly destabilise the hierarchies separating how IR debates pivot still on the duality between 'high' international politics and 'low' popular culture?

Whatever the response may be to this question, with all this cultural richness and cross-disciplinary sharing comes a note of caution about the twin perils of methodological parochialism and disciplinary hermeticism on the one hand and, on the other, a temptation to treat the arts and culture as ontologically distinct from other objects of analysis – that is to dis-embed these artefacts and practices from their also over-determined, changing socio-historical contexts. Sometimes this is through a quest to trump the mainstream with new transcendent categories of inquiry. Sometimes it is also the product of another mainstream and its critics, in this case that of western cultural criticism, art and literary theory.

As Ross (2011) reminds us above, bringing an aesthetic or cultural sensibility to a discipline such as IR, a discipline that has long eschewed either the relevance or formative influence of those domains deemed strictly-not-political, need not lead to mystifications in an attempt to present the merging of politics, art and culture as if such a merger in itself represents a shift up the epistemological food chain; another step forward in a quest for truth about how the world really works or not, as the case may be – for example, a civilisational or political failure in the fulfilment of certain ideas about modernity, enlightenment, cosmopolitan ideals, liberal democracy, and so on. Disciplinary border-crossings like musical collaborations work best as a reciprocal practice, or at least a two-way street.

Along these lines, arguments about politics and aesthetic theory notwithstanding (Bleiker 2012), one established approach to popular cultural references looks for mimetic illustrations of the 'international' in popular culture. Daniel Drezner (2015), for example, uses the notion of a zombie apocalypse to illustrate the different approaches taken by different schools of IR thought to explaining the behaviours of actors in the face of threat.

Another favourite line of inquiry is to consider how reconfigurations of vertically modelled local–national–international political dynamics are interpolated with changes in the practices, artefacts and global culture industries of the day. In these kinds of approach, music can be used as an empirical focus without broaching the musicological dimensions. Thus, for example, studies of cultural imperialism that look for cultural change in subordinate social formations in response to imperial or colonial pressures (Grayson, Davies and Philpott 2009); or investigations of how intellectual property regimes emerge in response to the 'piracy' of cultural products under the aegis of digital downloading and the global music industry and its respective dance and subcultures of sampling. From here, we see celebratory and concerned studies of hip-hop, DJ dance cultures and the appropriation of cultural heritage by savvy and creative western musicians where the quest for authenticity has replaced the critique of said authenticity (Adorno 2002).

Such an approach – one that treats the international as an independent variable and the cultural, such as music, as a dependent variable – remains valuable for understanding conventional international politics, ironically because:

(1) it highlights the ways in which the study – and practice – of the world politics/popular culture/everyday life nexus are contingent upon the interplay of their respective ways of doing things, knowledge-power relations and respective horizons of understanding; and

(2) it illustrates that cultural forms, including popular culture, are also shaped by the large-scale and localised political and economic concerns that continue to engage the on-going debates that differentiate the various schools of thought in International Relations as an academic discipline.

In this understanding, music can be incorporated without challenging these ways of conducting research – diehards who would keep the social and cultural world completely out of the equation notwithstanding. However, when we move into asking questions of a different, musicological order – such as 'What, or indeed where, are the international (or global) politics of music-making?' or 'How are world politics rendered musicologically?' – from an IR disciplinary perspective, we may find our analysis suffering from some important limitations.

The first of these is that, by its very nomenclature, *International Relations* is an epistemological given that posits the autonomy of inter-state relations over and above the practices and productions of the (popular) cultural realm. The prevailing ontologies and methodologies of IR remain intact in this respect, even when cogently critiqued or examined from other points of view (geographical, ethnic, gendered peripheries) or methodological choice (post-structuralist, constructivist, feminist, and so on).

Second, even if a critique of IR is implicitly or explicitly expressed in the ways the field takes up popular culture, then methodologically a prevailing positivist reflex tends to foreclose deeper explorations of the ontological foundations of the whole enterprise – based on literary and visual registers that validate the observer's power over the observed, the written over the sonically and kinetically experienced. Thus, even if said international, including its morphing into the global, is found to have negative effects in or consequences for cultural practice, and even if changes to governance and organisation are called for – as in Critical International Relations Theory – the international nevertheless *is*: and the ways the international distributes and locates the possibilities for political life remain over the horizon of critical expectations. In other words, in this understanding of the relation between music and world politics, there has been no 'musicking' of IR at all.

But what happens if we turn this refrain on its head? What if we investigate instead two sorts of questions that, while overlapping, are distinct in their methodological implications: 'What does, or could, world politics sound like?' and 'How does, or could, *the study of* world politics sound?' And by what means can we apprehend these politics of knowledge as and in sounds; rendered in recognisable forms of the classical or popular musical canon that have been unpacked and addressed by music scholars for their own silences and oversights (of gender, race, religion and class, for instance), or revised and reheard, thanks to mechanical and now digital forms of reproduction and (re-)creation?

To turn the inquiry around this way, IR scholarship into popular musical cultures, indeed into music as cultural practice more generally, needs to take more seriously the work done by musicologists and ethnomusicologists. Have scholars of world politics got the musicological tools of analysis on hand or, indeed, the will to engage with the 'new music research' literature (Franklin 2005, pp. 10-12) and debates? Are they willing to shift from the search for meaning to the qualities of music-as/and-sound that is not, and cannot, be bound by nation-state imaginaries and institutional assumptions (Miller 2008)? Are they willing to take the latter as constituent of a particular set of political questions for this century that has its roots in twentieth-century cultural and technological changes to how music is made, performed and consumed?

If the answer to the above questions is 'yes', namely that there is a rich vein of inquiry into the musical/musicological dimensions of world politics, then the task before us is to get closer to music scholars who have been considering the shifting politics of the musical forms, riffs, samples, ragas and performance traditions that are music research's objects of analysis. Or should a musical interest in the study of the popular culture and world politics nexus just accept at face value the non-musical dimensions to the appropriation or looting of a well-loved score being played over and over in the headphones of the tank drivers in a combat zone, or oozed into our semi-conscious in the elevators of the hotels hosting international events, or admire the sounds of music from home on the small radio in the 'illegal' migrant worker's carrier bag, which gives her some homely comfort in a hostile foreign city?

Where to put the remixed, electronic mash-ups of the music of the internet age or the singular and individualised creative enterprise based on inspiration, originality and the genial figure of the great (white, male) composer/DJ? Particularly since electronic music and its digital-era progeny, sampling, echoed arguments in literary theory that 'appropriation, mimicry, quotation, allusion, and sublimated collaboration consist of a kind of sine qua non of the creative act, cutting across all forms and genres in the realm of cultural production' (Lethem 2008, p. 29). It has been some time now since these and other musical myths were debunked within mainstream music research, ethnocentric and political economic predilections put in their place in the wake of feminist and ethnographic studies of how the rest of the world makes, and consumes, their music – how their music becomes refashioned as ours.

These sorts of questions remain open to debate within music studies, broadly defined even as they are under-theorised in IR circles for now. Political and technological changes over the last quarter century, at least, have established the ways in which digital musical cultures and creative industries have become established in popular and scholarly imaginaries. They provide the soundtracks for computer and video games, become source material for DJs and/or composers – and thereby point to ways in which these contemporary musical practices play with those of the past. This is where musicking (the study of) world politics articulates political closures and possibilities in turn.

In Conclusion

As Lee Hirsch notes, in his reflections on the importance of song and musical manifestations during times of intense national and transnational struggle through the prism of the anti-apartheid struggles of the black South African majority, the starting point is well measured already. Throughout history and across (musical) cultures, in 'many struggles worldwide, people have used music to give courage, to console, and to strengthen … . Song becomes a means to mobilise the masses by creating an electrifying climate for change' (Hirsch 2008, p. 217). The converse is also true in that history shows a variety of musical forms, compositions and means of transmission – indeed, sometimes the same one (the much-used Beethoven, for example, before, during and since the Nazi period) – have also been deployed to create 'an electrifying climate for change' (ibid.) for social and political forces of repression, genocidal programmes of destruction, and cultural revolutions. This is now a truism since *Resounding International Relations* was published. What we need now is to examine more closely how these sonorities operate on, and within, listening and receptive bodies, physical and communal.

What is more difficult to ascertain, and to keep situated in IR frames of reference, is how specifically the music provides a rich vein of analysis for scholars of world politics. Situating music in IR is a challenge, first, because the music itself evokes a host of musicological – that is, theoretical and methodological – issues and has its own scholarly literature (pointed to in our references). As Miller notes, similarly to many others, music 'is always a metaphor. It's an open signifier, an invisible, utterly malleable material. It's not fixed or cast in stone' (Miller 2004, pp. 20-21; see also Pasler 2008 and Miller 2008). A second reason is that music scholarship takes the analysis out of meta-/macro levels of analysis of international relations into the multiplex, micro-analytical frames of cultural studies, the formal concerns of (ethno)musicology, and the everyday practices and gendered power hierarchies of sociology and anthropology.

But we cannot embrace these opportunities without acknowledging the challenges: to (re) educate ourselves both musically and musicologically. We must broaden the analysis of music from its long-standing dependence on discovering the manifest or hidden content via lyrics or marketing genre. We need to acknowledge the problem of ethnocentrism and its twin, the exotification of music – meaning not only world music, but music as the Other. Our plea to consider method as a two-way street: International Relations as a theory of the problem of difference (Inayatullah and Blaney 2004), of bodies (Shepherd 2014), and with that of the audible world. To date, music/sound is still overlooked, constituent elements to explorations of what may or may not constitute the political in current debates. This two-way street also means taking into account the racial, gendered and geopolitical forces that position politico-musical differences as subordinate to the dominant key.

But while we engage our analyses with insights drawn from IR, we also seek to engage musicological language, literature and modes of analysis to consider the phenomenology of sound and the influences of emergent musical practices, such as digital, club cultures and remixing that in turn take their cues from the musicking of generations, and genres, past.

To end by looking back in order to move forward, a decade on from the conversations and musical sharing that were part of *Resounding International Relations*, we recall that this book was conceived as an invitation, an *opening* by all those who took part. By this we mean that moving out into the world of sound, of which music is one aspect, was an opening-up of the field as an increasingly multifaceted and multidisciplinary enterprise to new sources of material for reflection. But we also mean to enable an opening of the ears and aural sensibilities to the ways in which music research and musical practice can contribute to the study of world politics, a field that is still very much under construction in this century.

References

Adorno, T.W. (2002 [1938]) 'On the Fetish Character in Music and the Regression of Listening' in A. Arato and E. Gebhardt (eds), *The Essential Frankfurt School Reader*, New York: Continuum, 270-299.

Adorno, T.W. (2002) *Essays on Music*, selected and introduced by R. Leppert, London and New York: Routledge.

Appadurai, A. (2002). 'Disjuncture and Difference in the Global Cultural Economy' in J.X. Inda and R. Rosaldo (eds), *The Anthropology of Globalization: A Reader*, Massachusetts/Oxford: Blackwell, 46-64.

Attali, J. (1989) *Noise: The Political Economy of Music,* B. Massumi (trans.), Minneapolis: University of Minnesota Press.

Barenboim, D. and Said, E.W. (2003) *Parallels and Paradoxes: Explorations in Music and Society*, New York: Pantheon Books.

Barenboim, D. (2003) 'Germans, Jews and Music' in D. Barenboim and E.W. Said, *Parallels and Paradoxes: Explorations in Music and Society*, New York: Pantheon Books, 169-174.

Benjamin, W. (1970 [1936]) 'The Work of Art in the Age of Mechanical Reproduction' in *Illuminations*, London: Random House, 211-244.

Bennett, J. (2010) *Vibrant Matter: A Political Ecology of Things*, Durham, NC: Duke University Press.

Bennett, T., Frith, S., Grossberg, L., Shepherd, J. and Turner, G. (eds), 1993, *Rock and Popular Music: Politics, Policies, Institutions*, London and New York: Routledge.

Benson, B. (2003) *The Improvisation of Musical Dialogue: A Phenomenology of Music*, Cambridge and New York: Cambridge University Press.

Berger, K. (2007) *Bach's Cycle, Mozart's Arrow*, Berkley: University of California Press.

Bleiker, R. (2012) *Aesthetics and World Politics*, London and New York: Palgrave MacMillan.

Brown, R. (2005) 'Americanization at its Best? The Globalization of Jazz' in M.I. Franklin (ed.), *Resounding International Relations: On Music, Culture, and Politics*, Basingstoke: Palgrave MacMillan, 89-111.

Brown, C. (2008) *Politics in Music: Music and Political Transformation from Beethoven to Hip-Hop*, Farsight Press.

Carver, T. (2005) 'Operatic Mythologies, Political Performativity and Cinema: Visconti, Verdi and the Risorgimento' in M.I. Franklin (ed.), *Resounding International Relations: On Music, Culture, and Politics*, New York and London: Palgrave MacMillan, 223-238.

Certeau, M. de (1997) *Culture in the Plural,* Minneapolis: University of Minnesota Press.

Cox, R.W. (1981) 'Social Forces, States, and World Orders: Beyond International Relations Theory', *Millennium: Journal of International Studies*, 10(2): 126-155.

Crary, J. (1992) *Techniques of the Observer: On Vision and Modernity in the Nineteenth Century,* Cambridge, MA: MIT Press.

Cusick, S. (2006) 'Music as Torture/Music as a Weapon', *Sibetrans: Revista Transcultural de Música*, no. 10, <http://www.sibetrans.com/trans/articulo/152/music-as-torture-music-as-weapon> (accessed 22 January 2015).

Davies, M. (2005) '"Do It Yourself": Punk Rock and the Disalienation of International Relations' in M.I. Franklin (ed.), *Resounding International Relations: On Music, Culture, and Politics*, Basingstoke: Palgrave MacMillan, 113-140.

Drezner, D.W. (2015) *Theories of International Politics and Zombies*, revived edition, Princeton, NJ: Princeton University Press.

Dunn, K. (2008) 'Never Mind the Bollocks: The Punk Rock Politics of Global Communication', *Review of International Studies*, 34(1): 193-210.

Franklin, M.I. (2005) 'Resounding International Relations: Introductory Improvisations On A Theme' in M.I. Franklin (ed.), *Resounding International Relations: On Music, Culture, and Politics*, New York and London: Palgrave MacMillan, 1-26.

Franklin, M.I. (2013) 'Musical Sampling and the Cultural Geopolitics of Silence', paper presented at the Annual Convention of the International Studies Association, San Francisco: Panel SD24, World Politics and Diffusion: The Case of Popular Culture, 6 April 2013.

Gammon, E. (2008) 'Affect and the Rise of the Self-Regulating Market', *Millennium*, 37(2): 251-278.

Gay, P. (2007) *Modernism: The Lure of Heresy from Baudelaire to Beckett and Beyond*, London: Vintage Books.

Gilroy, P. (1993) *The Black Atlantic: Modernity and Double Consciousness*, Cambridge, MA: University of Harvard.

Goehr, L. (1994) 'Political Music and the Politics of Music' in P. Alperson (ed.) *Musical Worlds: New Directions in the Philosophy of Music*, Pennsylvania: Pennsylvania State University Press, 131-144.

Goldsmith, M. (2012) *Discord: The Story of Noise*, London and New York: Oxford University Press.

Grayson, K., Davies, M. and Philpott, S. (2009) 'Pop Goes IR? Researching the World Politics-Popular Culture Continuum', *Politics*, 29(3): 155-163.

Halbert, D. (2005) 'Sharing as Piracy: The Digital Future of Music' in M.I. Franklin (ed.), *Resounding International Relations: On Music, Culture, and Politics*, Basingstoke: Palgrave Macmillan: 71-88.

Henriques, J. (2008) 'Sonic Diaspora, Vibrations and Rhythm: Thinking through the sounding of the Jamaican dancehall session', *African and Black Diaspora*, 1(2): 215-236.

Henriques, J. (2010) 'The Vibrations of Affect and their Propagation on Night Out on Kingston's Dancehall Scene', *Body & Society*, 16(1): 57-89.

Hirsch, L. (2008) 'South Africa's Rhythms of Resistance' in Miller, P.D. (ed), *Sound Unbound: Sampling Digital Music and Culture*, Cambridge, MA and London: MIT Press, 215-218.

Horkheimer, M. and Adorno, T.W. (1972 [1947]) *Dialectic of Enlightenment*, J. Cumming (trans.), New York: Seabury Press.

Huntington, S.P. (1993) 'The Clash of Civilizations?', *Foreign Affairs*, 73(3): 22.

Inayatullah, N. and Blaney, D. (2004) *International Relations and the Problem of Difference*, London and New York: Routledge.

Inda, J.X. and Rosaldo, R. (eds) (2002) *The Anthropology of Globalization: A Reader*, Massachusetts and Oxford: Blackwell Publishers.

Korsyn, K. (2003) *Decentering Music: A Critique of Contemporary Musical Research*, New York: Oxford University Press.

Krims, A. (2000) *Rap Music and the Poetics of Identity*, Cambridge and New York: Cambridge University Press.

Lefebvre, H. (2004) *Rhythmanalysis: Space, Time, and Everyday Life*, London: Bloomsbury Academic.

Lethem, J. (2008) 'The Ecstasy of Influence: A Plagiarism Music' in Miller, P.D. (ed.) *Sound Unbound: Sampling Digital Music and Culture*, Cambridge MA, London UK: MIT Press, 25-52.

Lewis, G. E. (2008) 'Foreword' in J. Pasler, *Writing through Music: Essays on Music, Culture and Politics*, Oxford and New York: Oxford University Press, vii-xi.

Leys, R. (2011) 'The Turn to Affect: A Critique', *Critical Inquiry*, 37(3): 434-472.

Marcus, G. (1990) *Lipstick Traces: A Secret History of the Twentieth Century*, Cambridge, MA: Harvard University Press.

Miller, P.D. (2004) *Rhythm Science*, Cambridge MA: MIT Press.

Miller, P.D. (2008) 'In Through the Out Door: Sampling and the Creative Act' in Miller, P.D. (ed.), *Sound Unbound: Sampling Digital Music and Culture*, Cambridge MA, London UK: MIT Press, 5-20.

Mohaieman, N. (2008) 'Fear of a Muslim Planet; Hip-Hop's Hidden History' in Miller, P.D. (ed) *Sound Unbound: Sampling Digital Music and Culture*, Cambridge MA, London UK: MIT Press, 313-336.

Mowitt, J. (2002) *Percussion: Drumming, Beating, Striking*, Durham, NC and London: Duke University Press.

Negus, K. (1999) *Music Genres and Corporate Cultures*, London and New York: Routledge.

Pasler, J. (2008) *Writing through Music: Essays on Music, Culture and Politics*, Oxford, New York: Oxford University Press.

Rancière, J. (2009) *Aesthetics and Its Discontents*, Cambridge and Malden, MA: Polity Press.

Rancière, J. (2013) *The Politics of Aesthetics*, London and New York: Bloomsbury Academic.

Ridley, A. (2004) *The Philosophy of Music: Theme and Variations*, Edinburgh: Edinburgh University Press.

Ross, A. (2010) *The Rest is Noise: Listening to the Twentieth Century*, New York: Picador.

Ross, A. (2011) *Listen To This*, London: Fourth Estate.

Rumens, C. (2012) 'Pussy Riot's Punk Prayer is pure protest poetry', *The Guardian*, 20 August 2012, <http://www.theguardian.com/books/2012/aug/20/pussy-riot-punk-prayer-lyrics> (accessed 26 January 2015).

Said, E.W. (1992) *Musical Elaborations*, London: Vintage Books.

Said, E.W. (2001) 'The Clash of Ignorance', *The Nation*, 22 October 22, 2001, 1-5.

Said, E.W. (2006) *On Late Style: Music and Literature Against the Grain*, London: Bloomsbury.

Service, T. (2014) 'Symphony guide: Beethoven's Ninth ('Choral')', *The Guardian*, 9 September 2014, <http://www.theguardian.com/music/tomserviceblog/2014/sep/09/symphony-guide-beethoven-ninth-choral-tom-service> [accessed 26 January 2015].

Shaprio, M.J. (2004) *Methods and Nations: Cultural Governance and the Indigenous Subject*, London and New York: Routledge.

Shepherd, L.J. (2014) 'Sex or Gender? Bodies in Global Politics and Why Gender Matters' in Shepherd, L.J. (ed.) *Gender Matters in Global Politics: A Feminist Introduction to International Relations*, 2nd edition, London and New York: Routledge: 24-35.

Singer, P.W. and Friedman, A. (2014) *Cybersecurity and Cyberwar: What Everyone Needs to Know*, Oxford: Oxford University Press.

Small, C. (1998) *Musicking: The Meanings of Performing and Listening*, Hanover, NH: Wesleyan University Press.

Street, J. (2012) *Music and Politics*, Cambridge and Malden, MA: Polity Press.

Thrift, N. (2004) 'Intensities of Feeling: Towards a Spatial Politics of Affect', *Geografiska Annaler*, 86(1): 57-78.

Thompson, M. and Biddle, I. (eds) (2013) *Sound, Music, Affect: Theorizing Sonic Experience*, London: Bloomsbury.

Walker, R.B.J. (2010) *After the Globe, Before the World*, Abingdon: Routledge.

Waltz, K. (2001 [1954]) *Man, the State, and War: A Theoretical Analysis*, New York: Columbia University Press.

Weinrobe, P. and Inayatullah, N. (2005) 'A Medium of Others: Rhythmic Soundscapes as Critical Utopias', in M.I. Franklin (ed.), *Resounding International Relations: On Music, Culture, and Politics*, New York and London: Palgrave MacMillan: 239-262.

Wichelen, S. van (2005) '"My Dance Immoral? Alhamdulillah No!" Dangdut Music and Gender Politics in Contemporary Indonesia' in M.I. Franklin (ed.), *Resounding International Relations: On Music, Culture, and Politics*, New York and London: Palgrave MacMillan: 161-178.

Witkin, R.W. (1998) *Adorno on Music*, London and New York: Routledge.

Part Three

TEACHING POPULAR CULTURE AND WORLD POLITICS

Imperial Imaginaries: Employing Science Fiction to Talk about Geopolitics

ROBERT A. SAUNDERS
FARMINGDALE STATE COLLEGE

Popular culture is finding ever-greater purchase in the International Relations (IR) classroom. This is a reflection of the wealth of recent scholarship linking IR and geopolitics to popular culture, but also a realisation on the part of instructors that their students possess a helpful fluency in popular culture. This skill set allows for the employment of an intellectual shorthand that accelerates learning, facilitates critical analysis, and enables thoughtful discussions and debate. In this article, I will discuss the ways in which the genre of science fiction (sf) can be utilised to engage with the subject of geopolitics and, more specifically, imperial geopolitics. While the main focus of this piece is on pedagogy, I will also comment on current research trends in critical IR/popular geopolitics and how scholarly work on the popular culture-world politics continuum (Grayson et al. 2009) scaffolds what occurs in the (pop) IR classroom.

Sf is a genre of *space* (terrain, topography, 'zones', etc.), as well as *outer space*. With few exceptions, sf deals with questions of exploration (of territory), exploitation (of resources) and control (of others, usually via technology). Consequently, there is an explicit link to imperialism, defined as 'the maintenance (or expansion) of national power at the expense of other, less empowered, countries through methods of governance at a distance' (Dittmer 2010, p. 55). It has been argued that sf – especially the most dominant subgenre of sf, tales of extraterrestrial voyages and encounters – emerged as a response to the effective end of terrestrial conquest, i.e. the end of (Western) imperial expansion (see, for instance, Rieder 2008). We know that when Alexander saw the breadth of his domain, he wept, for there were no more worlds to conquer; however, 'having no place on Earth left for the radical exoticism of unexplored territory,' nineteenth-century writers – ersatz imperialists of the imagination – simply 'invented places elsewhere' (Rieder 2008, p. 4).

These imperial imaginaries took many forms, from Edgar Rice Burroughs' 'Mars' to Jules Verne's 'inner Earth' to H. G. Wells' 'Earth A.D. 802,701'. Throughout the twentieth century, the links between sf and colonisation only intensified; according to Csicsery-Ronay, '[t]he dominant sf nations are precisely those that attempted to expand beyond their national borders in imperial projects: Britain, France, Germany, Soviet Russia, Japan and the US' (2003, p. 231). Sf then not only reflects imperial ideology, it is also the product of it.

Science Fiction: Ideology, Identity, and Imperialism

With the advent of the Cold War, sf steadily morphed into a medium for global ideological contestation and identity negotiation, while comfortably retaining many of its imperialist connotations. As Dittmer (2010) points out, *Star Trek*, one of the most successful sf franchises of the past century, scripted an intergalactic competition between a peace-loving 'federation' (the US and its NATO allies) and a war-mongering 'empire' (the USSR and its Eastern Bloc satellites). As popular culture, such representations of place, space and people – especially through allegory – serve as a form of propaganda, or at least a kind of ideological pedagogy. The relationship between (imperial) geopolitics and sf arguably reached its apex in the first years of the Reagan administration, when the former B-movie actor-turned-leader of the 'free world' began to label the Soviet Union the 'Evil Empire' while touting his 'Star Wars' Strategic Defense Initiative (SDI). In fact, both discursive devices made use of the enormous cultural resonance of George Lucas' space operas *A New Hope* (1977) and *The Empire Strikes Back* (1980), thus affirming the world politics– popular culture nexus in the context of Mutually Assured Destruction (Kramer 1999).

Since the end of the Cold War and the implementation of the Global War on Terror (GWOT), sf has adapted to the realities of this new world order, continuing to interrogate questions of imperial power but with an increasingly postmodern geopolitical eye. This subtle shift has attracted the interest of IR scholars, with representative examples including how *Battlestar Galactica* interpolated 9/11 and the US occupation of Iraq (Buzan 2010; Kiersey and Neumann 2013), the role of *Doctor Who* in shaping British post-imperial engagement with its various 'Others' (Dixit 2012; Gupta 2013), and how the explosion of zombie sf functioned as a manifestation of globalised fear of uncontrolled borders (May 2010; Morrissette 2014).

While there are many similarities between the literary-political discourses of Cold War sf and its GWOT equivalent (particularly the notions of securitisation and the preservation of 'freedom'), it is important to recognise one important shift since the turn of the millennium: the competition between 'globalisation' (*read* neoliberalism) and 'localisation' (*read* autarky) has come to the fore (see Barber, 1996). As this competition between globalism and localism becomes increasingly important in the larger framework of neo-imperial geopolitics, sf – with its (potentially) critical examination of exploration, exploitation, and technology – allows for innovative tools and techniques in IR pedagogy.

Science Fiction as a Genre

Science fiction is the genre of the unknown, but imaginable, and as a result 'contemplates possible futures' (Gunn 2014, p. 34). Through its 'roots in the practice of philosophical speculation', sf is 'eminently constructive' in addressing questions that a given society is just beginning to ask, whether these are related to revolutionary change, imperial decay, environmental disaster, or impending dystopia (Paik 2010, p. 2). Furthermore, sf can 'mediate real social dilemma through imaginary resolutions' (Csicsery-Ronay 2003, p. 234), thus making the case for exposing potential opinion leaders in the field of IR to the questions it addresses. The genre also has a long history of using allegory to critique the actions of political elites, at both national and international level.

Speaking generally of all post-9/11 'geopolitical popular culture' (Purcell et al. 2010), the pro-hegemony orientation of mainstream visual media (films, television programmes, video games) typically serve to reinforce notions of a besieged, freedom-loving 'West' (a common refrain of the Bush-Blair administrations), while other platforms (novels, comic books/graphic novels and popular music) may provide a more nuanced approach to issues of geo-power *or* function as pillars of hegemony. Science fiction – a genre that is prevalent across many of these media platforms – arguably allows for a greater level of ideological elasticity than other geopolitically inclined genres, such as action-thrillers, spy fiction or (transnational) crime drama.

Given that sf is often allegorical in nature, these works of popular culture more easily allow for alternative readings. Comparing sf to the Bourne films (2002-2012) or the television series *24* (2001-2010), for example, it is much easier to prompt readings 'across' the text, as well as 'against' the text, in addition to reading 'with' the text (see Unsworth 2011). Thus, sf can be employed as a gateway to examining imperial geopolitics from a critical perspective, allowing students to interrogate the content at some distance and developing skills to address agency, representation, intertextuality and discourse analysis. Needless to say, most students also find the use of popular culture in the classroom make for a more 'interesting' experience, a non-trivial issue in current era of higher education's move towards the 'student as customer'.

Teaching Imperial Geopolitics through Science Fiction

Specific to the subfield of imperial geopolitics, sf speaks truth to power just as easily as it reinforces existing hegemonies (and in some cases, imagines new ones). As a genre 'obsessed with colonialism and imperial adventure', sf frequently inverts the genuine threat that Euro-American imperialism has posed to the non-white peoples of the world, presenting instead an imaginary realm where 'white people' are threatened with subjugation or annihilation by a hostile alien force; although it is important to note that a significant portion of sf can be read as anti-colonial in nature (Berlatsky 2014). Consequently, the instructor seeking to promote learning outcomes that critically assess questions of power and privilege must tread lightly when using sf. Regardless of the political orientation of the texts, sf represents a deep reservoir for probing the vagaries of imperial geopolitics, and – if used properly – opens the door to sophisticated analysis of international relations and geopolitics in the classroom.

Why do students study IR? The reasons and rationales are legion: to further career plans in government service/transnational industry/NGOs, to pursue an advanced degree in the field, to learn a bit more about how the 'world actually works', to fulfill a degree requirement, or simply because the course fits one's schedule. My IR/geopolitics teaching experience is a roughly equal mix between US undergraduates who are pursuing non-related degrees (STEM fields, criminal justice, professional communications, etc.) and predominantly US graduate students who are more focused on the practical applications of the discipline (policy-making, military affairs, etc.). Given that the latter population tends to have a solid grounding in the inner workings of geopolitics, I will be focusing my analysis on the former group (full disclosure: as a researcher operating in the subfield of 'popular geopolitic', I am more prone to the use of popular culture in my lectures than others teaching the same subject matter).

Over the past decade I have developed a number of tactics and strategies for engaging these students in substantive discussions and debates on complex topics associated with the history of imperialism, geopolitical thinking and the relationship between territory, space and power. During this period, the vast majority of these students have shared a common foundational experience with IR: their first experience with foreign affairs – and the outside world more generally – was 9/11. Given this important reality, sf narratives of extraterritorial, even existential, threats from alien realms beyond the ken of the 'everyday American' tend to provoke strong emotions. With this emotion comes the opportunity to engage in productive analyses of popular-culture renderings of 'geo-power', i.e. how symbolic geographies, agents and objects are 'arranged, presented and projected' in such a way that they reinforce or tear down 'power-knowledge relations' in the contemporary world (Ó Tuathail 1996, p. 10).

Science Fiction Cinema and the IR/Geopolitics Classroom

Film analysis is perhaps the most common form of bringing sf into the IR/geopolitics classroom. Cinema allows for greater emotional effect than would be possible through standard approaches to teaching geopolitics and also levels the playing field for discussions, establishing a space where debate and exchange of ideas can occur more readily. Students are typically well versed in the aesthetic and political underpinnings of the medium of cinema, having been exposed to introductory elements of film theory in a variety of courses (modern languages, sociology, etc.).

As Weber points out, instructors also benefit from the growing sophistication of the Gen-Y and millennials' fluency in 'visual culture', which she argues is primarily autodidactic. Writing in 2001, she states, 'Not only do I find that the current generation of eighteen- to twenty-year-olds are better readers and writers of visual images than I am, I also find that they understand how to approach these media critically' (Weber 2001, p. 282). Yoking these skills to in-class film analysis can thus prove fruitful, though not without its own pitfalls. In addition to Weber, a number of IR instructors have penned essays about their own 'filmic IR' experiences in the classroom (Webber 2005; Nexon and Neumann 2006; Ruane and James 2008; Engert and Spencer 2009); however, I do not wish to recapitulate that analysis here. Instead, I will focus on a rather narrow subset of such pedagogy: using sf to 'talk about' imperial geopolitics in a critical way.

Most students, whether or not they are fans of sf, are generally familiar with the franchises and narrative arcs of *Star Trek* (1966-) and *Star Wars* (1977-). Given this resonance, I often use these media to open my lectures on imperial geopolitics. In class discussions about *Star Wars*, I challenge students to make connections between the films and geopolitics in the context of the Second Cold War and Global War on Terror. Whereas most students will naturally identify the US with the 'Rebel Alliance' of the first three films (typically in the context of the American Revolution) and the 'Empire' with the Soviet Union, I also challenge this reading by encouraging debates on core-periphery geopolitics (Flint 2001), specifically assessing the imperial might of the United States and the various systems of global governance Washington introduced in the post-WWII era. This critical analysis of the *Pax Americana* and other forms of neoliberal hegemony via sf typically begins as light-hearted foray into the fantastic, but can be quickly and effectively converted into a girding for asking serious questions about US foreign policy in places like the Philippines, the Congo and Chile.

Using the second triad of *Star Wars* films (1999-2005), I encourage students to excavate the geopolitics of the Separatist Alliance versus the Galactic Republic. I also ask my students to evaluate the geopolitical overtones of (the once-and-future Darth Vader) Anakin Skywalker's statement to his former mentor, Obi-Wan Kenobi, 'If you're not with me, you're my enemy', showing the scene alongside George W. Bush's post-9/11 Manichaean admonition to his allies and enemies alike that 'either you are with us, or you are with the terrorists'. *Star Trek* – generally accepted as a pop-culture paean to 'peaceful exploration' – can be read *with* the text, providing an entry point for discussing the geopolitical alliances of NATO (qua the United Federation of Planets) and the Warsaw Pact (qua the Klingon or Romulan empires); alternatively, students can be challenged to read either *across* or *against* the text to assess the neo-colonial actions of 'Starfleet' (employing the Star Trek tropes of 'First Contact', the 'Neutral Zone', etc.), as well as embedded hierarchies of 'race' via relations between the various 'species' with the Federation.

While problematic, it is also possible to introduce Said's (1979) concept of Orientalism in discussions of how the Federation (led by its mostly white humans) imagines alien zones like the Klingon Homeworld or the hive-like Borg vessels. While it is logistically impossible to encompass the ideological evolution of the Star Trek franchise over the past half-century (see Weldes 1999), I do provide a brief analysis of how changing orientations of the series towards geopolitical conquest and international conflict ground the students in the ways world politics influences popular culture (as well as the reverse), e.g. the making of peace with the Klingons in *Star Trek VI: The Undiscovered Country* (1991) and reimagining of Khan as a terrorist in *Star Trek: Into Darkness* (2013). The goal of employing these pop-culture products to talk about geo-power is not to produce an objective understanding of George Lucas' or Gene Roddenberry's galactic realms, but instead to promote intersubjective and intertextual knowledge, which in turn enables students to develop their geopolitical vocabulary and apply it to the real world.

Other popular sf films also address normative questions associated with (neo)imperial geopolitics. While overly simplistic in its representations of colonisation and resource exploitation, James Cameron's *Avatar* (2009) does offer the IR student a filmic perspective on Western imperial disregard for the lifeways, knowledge and natural environments of indigenous peoples. Neill Blomkamp's *District 9* (2009) is even more useful as a tool for engaging issues of the politics of colonial space, the discourse of 'going native', the sexualised politics of empire, and mediatisation of extreme 'Otherness'; given the film's setting in South Africa, the allegory of apartheid is extremely powerful inter-generation tool for connecting the experiences of the instructor (who likely remembers apartheid) to the student (likely born after its demise). The reboot of the television series *Battlestar Galactica* (2003-2009) is also a useful vehicle for critically interrogating the 'reassertion of imperial reason' (Slater 2011) following the US-led invasions of Afghanistan and Iraq, especially through the series' quasi-valorisation of suicide terrorism as tool of asymmetrical warfare. Through the use of active learning-style debates on these subjects, sf becomes a doorway for analysis, synthesis and evaluation of real-world geopolitical outcomes. As Engert and Spencer (2009) point out, film (and its small-screen cousin TV) enables students engage with issues, events, identities and narratives in IR and geopolitics. By focusing on sf, which imagines potential realities, students can be encouraged to see territorial power and geopolitics in a new light, making it easier for these students to subsequently critique the normative orientations of neo-imperial geopolitical thinkers they will be assigned to read in the course (including Zbigniew Brzezinski, Robert Kaplan and Parag Khanna).

The Pedagogical Value of the SF Novel

Use of visual media, however, is not the only method for incorporating popular culture into study of geopolitics. Personally, the sf novel has proved a valuable pedagogical resource, and one which promotes deeper engagement with the highly complex issues in changing geopolitical structure. Frank Herbert's *Dune* (1965), 'a multi-faceted struggle between an archaic, feudal, and ossified galactic Imperium and a vital, meritocratic, and adaptable desert people' (DiTommaso 2007, p. 269), remains a seminal text for such pedagogy, especially when introducing IR students to Machiavellian geopolitics (see Mulcahy 1996); however, I have also used the anti-imperialist cartographies of China Miéville's fiction to precipitate debates about Britain's imperial past and 'progressive' geopolitical alternatives.

Additionally, I have employed Paolo Bacigalupi's *The Windup Girl* (2009) to introduce students to the quasi-imperial geo-economic power of transnational corporations (see Luttwak 1990).

Based on my own scholarship on the geopolitics of zombiism (Saunders 2012; Saunders 2013), and making use of the growing pedagogical literature on bringing zombies into the IR classroom (Drezner 2011; Blanton 2013; Hannah and Wilkinson 2014), I frequently assign my students Max Brooks' *World War Z* (2006) (WWZ). Unlike the 2013 film, WWZ, appropriately subtitled *An Oral History of the Zombie War*, presents a cornucopia of critical geopolitical themes, including derisive assessments of Chinese relations with sub-Saharan Africa, the US embargo on Cuba and the United Nations' (in)capacity for global governance. Resulting from the current 'zombie turn' in popular culture (and IR scholarship), the walking dead provide an excellent foray into questions of securitisation, counter-terrorism and environmental security, all key topics that can be linked back to neo-imperial geopolitical visions and codes, as well as power structures that have been implemented since the end of the Cold War.

I will end on a cautionary note by assessing the potential risks of employing sf as tool for talking about imperial geopolitics. As a literary genre deeply imbricated in the projection of imperial power, sf presents a double-edged sword for instructors seeking to promote critical geopolitics in the IR classroom. While effective readings across and against texts can promote critical thinking, there is the constant risk that sf readings will serve to reinforce existing stereotypes, marginalise counter-hegemonic readings of the past and essentialise non-Western peoples and spaces (Hannah and Wilkinson 2014). Yet despite such caveats, sf presents a powerful medium for engaging students in critical analysis of imperial geopolitics.

References

Barber, B.R. (1996) *Jihad vs. McWorld: How Globalism and Tribalism are Reshaping the World,* New York: Ballantine Books.

Berlatsky, N. (2014) 'Why Sci-Fi Keeps Imagining the Subjugation of White People', *The Atlantic*, <http://www.theatlantic.com/entertainment/archive/2014/2004/why-sci-fi-keeps-imagining-the-enslavement-of-white-people/361173/>.

Blanton, R.G. (2013) 'Zombies and International Relations: A Simple Guide for Bringing the Undead into Your Classroom', *International Studies Perspectives*, 14(1): 1-13.

Brooks, M. (2006) *World War Z: An Oral History of the Zombie War,* New York: Three Rivers Press.

Buzan, B. (2010) 'America in Space: The International Relations of *Star Trek* and *Battlestar Galactica*', *Millennium: Journal of International Studies*, 39(1): 175-180.

Csicsery-Ronay, I. (2003) 'Science Fiction and Empire', *Science Fiction Studies*, 30(2): 231-245.

DiTommaso, L. (2007) 'The Articulation of Imperial Decadence and Decline in Epic Science Fiction', *Extrapolation*, 48: 267-292.

Dittmer, J. (2010) *Popular Culture, Geopolitics, and Identity,* Lanham, MD: Rowman & Littlefield.

Dixit, P. (2012) 'Relating to Difference: Aliens and Alienness in Doctor Who and International Relations', *International Studies Perspectives*, 13(3): 289-306.

Drezner, D.W. (2011) *Theories of International Politics and Zombies*, Princeton and Oxford: Princeton University Press.

Engert, S. and Spencer, A. (2009) 'International Relations at the Movies: Teaching and Learning about International Politics through Film', *Perspectives*, 17(1): 83-104.

Flint, C. (2001) 'The Geopolitics of Laughter and Forgetting: A World-Systems Interpretation of the Post-Modern Geopolitical Condition', *Geopolitics*, 6(3): 1-16.

Grayson, K., Davies, M. and Philpott, S. (2009) 'Pop Goes IR? Researching the Popular Culture World Politics Continuum', *Politics*, 29(3): 155-163.

Gunn, E. (2014) 'Brave New Words', *Smithsonian*, 45(2): 34-37.

Gupta, A. (2013) '*Doctor Who* and Race: Reflections on the Change of Britain's Status in the International System', *Round Table*, 102(1): 41-50.

Hannah, E. and Wilkinson, R. (2014) 'Zombies and IR: A Critical Reading', *Politics*. Available online, <http://onlinelibrary.wiley.com/doi/10.1111/1467-9256.12077/full [accessed 30 March 2015].

Kiersey, N.J. and Neumann, I.B. (2013) *Battlestar Galactica and International Relations*, London: Routledge.

Kramer, P. (1999) 'Star Wars', *History Today*, 49(3): 41-46.

Luttwak, E. (1990) 'From Geopolitics to Geoeconomics: Logic of Conflict, Grammar of Commerce', *The National Interest*, 20 (Summer): 17-23.

May, J. (2010) 'Zombie Geographies and the Undead City', *Social & Cultural Geography*, 11(3): 285-298.

Morrissette, J.J. (2014) 'Zombies, International Relations, and the Production of Danger: Critical Security Studies versus the Living Dead', *Studies in Popular Culture*, 36(2): 1-28.

Mulcahy, K. (1996) '*The Prince* on Arrakis: Frank Herbert's Diaiogue with Machiavelli', *Extrapolation*, 37(1): 22-36.

Nexon, D.H. and Neumann, I.B. (2006) H*arry Potter and International Relations*, Lanham, MD: Rowman & Littlefield.

Ó Tuathail, G. (1996) *Critical Geopolitics*, Abingdon, UK: Taylor & Francis.

Paik, P.Y. (2010) *From Utopia to Apocalypse: Science Fiction and the Politics of Catastrophe*, Minneapolis and London: University of Minnesota Press.

Purcell, D., Scott Brown, M. and Gokmen, M. (2010) 'Achmed the Dead Terrorist and Humor in Popular Geopolitics', *Geoforum*, 75: 373-385.

Rieder, J. (2008) *Colonialism and the Emergence of Science Fiction*, Middletown, CT: Wesleyan University Press.

Ruane, A.E. and James, P. (2008) 'The International Relations of Middle-earth: Learning from *Lord of the Rings*', *International Studies Perspectives*, 9(4): 377-394.

Said, E. (1979) *Orientalism*, New York: Vintage Books.

Saunders, R.A. (2012) 'Undead Spaces: Fear, Globalisation, and the Popular Geopolitics of Zombiism', *Geopolitics*, 17(1): 80-104.

Saunders, R.A. (2013) 'Zombies in the Colonies: Imperialism and Contestation of Ethno-Political Space in Max Brooks' *The Zombie Survival Guide*', in Montin, S. and Tsitas, E. (eds) *Monstrous Geographies: Places and Spaces of the Monstrous*, Oxford: Inter-Disciplinary Press, 19-46.

Slater, D. (2011) 'The Imperial Present and the Geopolitics of Power', *Geopolitics*, 1(1): 191-205.

Unsworth, L. (2011) *Multimodal Semiotics: Functional Analysis in Contexts of Education*, London and New York: Continuum.

Webber, J. (2005) '*Independence Day* as a Cosmopolitan Moment: Teaching International Relations', *International Studies Perspectives*, 6(3): 374-392.

Weber, C. (2001) 'The Highs and Lows of Teaching IR Theory: Using Popular Films for Theoretical Critique', *International Studies Perspectives*, 2(3): 281-287.

Weldes, J. (1999) 'Going Cultural: Star Trek, State Action, and Popular Culture', *Millennium: Journal of International Studies*, 28(1): 117-134.

The Challenges of Teaching Popular Culture and World Politics

KYLE GRAYSON
NEWCASTLE UNIVERSITY

Introduction

Over the past three decades, the discipline of International Relations has widened to include concerns beyond the Waltzian holy trinity of the man, the state and war. It has also deepened to incorporate forms of analysis that are more probing of the political than the neo-neo synthesis or the polite face of constructivism that this synthesis has regurgitated. One of the consequences of the growing pluralism of the field has been the development of the popular culture–world politics continuum (Davies, Grayson and Philpott 2009) for both pedagogical and enquiry-driven aims. While there is an emerging literature on using artefacts of popular culture and cultural methods for assessment (Earnest and Fish 2014) in the International Relations seminar room, there has been very little examination of the challenges of teaching popular culture as an important constitutive element of world politics in its own right. In this article, I attempt to address this gap by drawing upon my own experiences as both a researcher and teacher of popular culture and world politics.

Why Do I Use Popular Culture?

I am primarily interested in how ideas, modes of interpretation, discourses, representations, and affects circulate and resonate across the continuum formed by popular culture and world politics. And part of the interest lies in being humble about the fact that I am still not precisely sure what popular culture and world politics entail. Thus, I remain receptive to new ways of understanding their connections, impacts, location, processes of production, distribution and consumption, as well as their audiences and modes of interpretation.

Popular culture is an important site where our understandings of the world, politics and identity are formed, contested and (re)formed. It produces imaginative geographies that orientate audiences, as well as emotional attachments and enmities that shape what is considered to be politically possible and desirable. Popular culture can serve as a *lingua franca*, connecting global audiences to local disputes, and contribute to discursive formations shaping debates from drone warfare (Grayson 2014a)[1] to intellectual property rights. Moreover, the material artefacts (Salter 2015) of popular culture themselves – such as mobile phones, fashion, the internet or food – are imbricated within global supply chains, distribution networks, patterns of consumption, and relations of power. Thus, given the prominence of popular culture in world politics, I would find it amiss to omit it from the teaching of international relations.

---

[1] Grayson, K. (2014) 'Drones and Video Games', E-International Relations, <http://www.e-ir. info/2014/02/25/drones-and-video-games/>.

Key Challenges

Of course, it is one thing to claim the importance of a topic area and quite another to demonstrate that importance to students through pedagogical practice. Popular culture and world politics is no different in this regard. While some of the challenges that arise from teaching popular culture are not unique – for example, getting students to engage with the required reading – others either manifest themselves differently or are distinctive to this topic area. Drawing on my past decade of teaching and researching at the intersections of popular culture and world politics, the following challenges come to the front on my mind in terms of pedagogic practice.

What Are You Trying to Achieve?

All courses have specific learning aims and objectives that drive how they are taught. But within the remit of International Relations, there are at least four ways that popular culture can be used in the seminar room. Three of these analyse world politics through popular culture, while the fourth attempts to understand popular culture through world politics.

The first way is to read world politics through popular culture by using artefacts as allegorical devices to understand conceptual, theoretical, methodological and/or historical material. This is by far the most common way (Ruane and James 2008) in which popular culture is mobilised within International Relations teaching. Within this configuration, popular culture is a supplemental tool for conveying more orthodox International Relations subjects, rather than an object of study in its own right. For example, Cindy Weber (2014) has written an excellent textbook that uses film as a way of unpacking the assumptions underpinning theories of International Relations, while Daniel Drezner (2009) has used the conceit of a zombie apocalypse to introduce students to theoretical traditions in the field. The unfortunate downside is that using popular culture as a supplement can feed into narrow conceptions (Hannah and Wilkinson 2014) of what world politics is and what is important to the field of International Relations.

A second way is to analyse international relations aesthetically (Bleiker 2001). In this configuration, artefacts of popular culture are deployed to provide alternative readings of world politics by focusing on their representations, affects and embodied practices. For example, Michael J. Shapiro (2010) has argued that films such as *Devil in a Blue Dress* are able to show how historically constructed racial orders – largely missed by orthodox approaches to international relations (Vitalis 2000) – are revealed through the bodily comportment of the film's main characters. Similarly, there has been work undertaken on the weaponisation of sound, including using music to torture (Cusick 2006) and rhythm as means to produce feelings of rage that are conducive to acts of violence (Protevi 2010).

A third way is to treat artefacts of popular culture as vernacular theorisations of world politics (McLaughlin 1998) that either promote hegemonic understandings of international relations or produce counter-hegemonic understandings of the status quo. For example, Nick Robinson (2015) has recently explored the ambiguous role of American exceptionalism in video games, while Andrew Boulton (2008) has analysed the imaginative geographies of country music in the aftermath of 9/11.

A fourth way is to reverse the direction of analysis and read popular culture thorough world politics. The primary aim here is to be able to find answers to the question: what can world politics tell us about popular culture? This can include explorations of the forms of cultural production and commercialisation underpinning global relations of power (Lisle and Pepper 2005), the use of metaphors and tropes (Grayson 2014) by key actors that draw from popular culture, how specific modes of cultural interpretation are distributed globally (Mathijs 2006), and how world politics provides affective and/or phenomenological dynamics that shape popular culture (Altheide 2006).

Each of these readings provides a slightly different emphasis along the popular culture–world politics continuum. Thus, how one wishes to connect popular culture and world politics is going to affect how a course is structured, the readings that are selected, the kinds of artefacts that are used, and the ways in which seminar time is organised.

How to Structure the Course?

For many topic areas in International Relations there are tried and tested course structures that have been deployed over several generations to present introductory and advanced-level treatments. Even for those who wish to do things differently, there is, at least, a norm to be rebutted. Teaching the popular culture–world politics continuum, though, is largely *tabula rasa* in terms of structure. It could be done thematically, for example through traditional international relations topic areas (e.g. nuclear war), more diffuse but pertinent subjects (e.g. the politics of belonging), or genres from within popular culture (e.g. hip-hop). One could also structure a course by medium (for example, radio, television, film, music, literature, food) or by thinkers/key texts (for example, Stuart Hall, Walter Benjamin, Jacques Rancière, *To Seek Out New Worlds* [Weldes 2003]). Method provides another way of arranging a course by having sections that speak to specific ways of analysing the popular culture-world politics continuum (for example, semiotics, discourse analysis or narratology).

Again, what will work best is going to depend on what you are trying to achieve more broadly and what you wish to emphasise within the popular culture–world politics continuum. From past practice, I have found that the further I have moved away from what will be immediately received by students as textual or visual towards other sensibilities like sound, touch, taste and feeling, the more pedagogically rewarding the experience has become. For example, in a MA-level course, I lead a week on hip-hop where the focus is on how this medium has developed a sonic landscape in conjunction with Islam – beginning in the United States, but more recently in North Africa. Rather than focus on the immediate lyrical content, students are encouraged to explore what they are hearing (e.g. beats, melodies, timbre, tone, voice, patterns of rhyme) and how it has been produced (e.g. drum machines, sampling) in order to unpack the ways in which forms of power and resistance circulate globally.

Moving Beyond the Allegorical?

My experience has been that getting students to analyse the popular culture-world politics continuum beyond allegorical connections that may link artefacts and international relations is a considerable challenge. Moreover, recent research (Holland 2014) has suggested that weaker students may even struggle to understand very simple metaphors that might bind an artefact (for example, the book *World War Z*) to issues like migration. However, this is not to say that one should not try; what this does mean is that one needs to be realistic about what students will initially be capable of undertaking.

Know Your Students

A common mistake when teaching popular culture and world politics is to overestimate the skill set that students will bring with them into the course. Students will likely not be as culturally aware or technologically savvy as typical media reporting would lead you to believe. Thus, it is important not to make assumptions about cultural knowledge or the ability of students to navigate – or have access to – specific technologies, content delivery mechanisms or media forms.

Similarly, students will initially lack the conceptual or methodological tools to provide analyses of cultural artefacts beyond the identification of reflective similarities in content to events they already identify as being 'international relations'. This can make it difficult to push students beyond conventional accounts of what world politics might be. The challenge may be even more pronounced in educational contexts like the UK, where students begin to specialise prior to university and may have very little background in the arts and humanities or any form of methods training beyond an introductory research skills class. Thus, as in other parts of the International Relations curriculum, it can be a struggle to get students to develop and apply conceptual and methodological material. This can be compounded by a sense that 'anything goes' when it comes to analysing popular culture. Thus, it can take a considerable amount of effort and determination as a teacher to get students to understand that while there may be many approaches to analysing popular culture and world politics, each has a set of requirements for analytic rigour that should be met.

There is also a tendency to underestimate the unconventional social dynamics that may arise in the classroom. Our identities and political subjectivities are very much imbricated into our practices of cultural consumption (Warde 2005), including our likes and dislikes. Moreover, within social groupings, being a cultural taste-maker (that is, an individual who discovers interesting cultural content before other group members) can be a desirable position. However, the classroom is not the place for you to undertake this role. It is important to remember that students are unlikely to share similar ideas of 'cool' amongst themselves, let alone with you.

In more participatory or problem-based classroom contexts this may mean that students are reticent to draw upon their own experiences (e.g. as gamers) or bring in artefacts for analysis out of a fear that they will be judged by peers and classified accordingly. Thus, it is important to create an environment where students feel secure in taking risks knowing that even if these do not pay off, there will be no lingering judgments regarding what it says about them as a person. It also helps to have thick skin yourself for those times in which your own tastes are exposed as being ridiculously naff.

Forms of Assessment?

As a subject area, popular culture and world politics lends itself to alternative modes of assessment, such as videos, song writing, painting, literature, dance, comics, programming, and so on, and many who teach in this area encourage students to submit work for assessment that goes beyond the standard 10-20 page research paper. While this is laudable, anecdotal evidence suggests that most students prefer to stay within the comfort zone of familiar assessment types. This is particularly the case in systems – like the UK – where a single form of assessment may be worth between 50-100 per cent of the final course grade. Thus, students often do not want to take the gamble of attempting unfamiliar tasks for credit.

If you are interested in pushing the frontiers of assessment in International Relations and having student buy-in, it may therefore be valuable to provide a safety net of sorts, such as a reflective essay on what the student hoped to show with the alternative assessment, whether it met the initial aims – and if not, why it may have fallen short – and what was learned about popular culture and world politics through the creative process itself. It is also worth considering what alternative forms will be assessing in relation to the learning aims and objectives of the course, and whether you have the same competencies to assess a mash-up video or photographic exhibition as you would a standard research paper.

Lessons Learned?

In teaching popular culture and politics, there are two final lessons I have learned. The first is that while it involves a considerable amount of preparation in terms of gathering appropriate artefacts, the most effective means of teaching the popular culture–world politics continuum from my experience has been to organise classroom time such that the focus is on applying theoretical and conceptual insights to the analysis of cultural artefacts using specific methods.

For example, as part of an initiative that involves video-linked teaching between Newcastle University in the UK and York University in Canada, we have had students compare the opening ceremonies to the 2010 Winter Olympic Games in Vancouver[2] and the 2012 Summer Olympic Games in London,[3] paying particular attention to the narratives running through these spectacles. To apply the concept of the male gaze, I have had students conduct semiotic analyses of beer adverts. To explore practices of memorialisation and erasure that are central to the re-emergence of imperialist nostalgia (Rosalndo 1989) within England, we have sent students around the Newcastle area to look at war memorials and other forms of commemoration[4] that dot the urban landscape. Thus, orientating a module towards problem-based/experiential learning by building up student skills on a weekly basis towards a final project or outcome can be a particularly rewarding way of teaching the popular culture and world politics continuum.

I have been relatively lucky in terms of the levels of resistance I have received from colleagues, university managers and external examiners – who may be more orthodox in their understanding of international relations – with respect to teaching popular culture. But when resistance did emerge, a second lesson that I quickly learned was that the terms 'pilot project' and 'advanced research methods training' can provide a lot of cover for heterodox approaches to the field of International Relations and pedagogy within the UK context.

---

[2] olympicvancouver2010, 'Complete Vancouver 2010 Opening Ceremony', YouTube, < https://www. youtube.com/watch?v=MxZpUueDAvc>

[3] Olympics, 'Opening Ceremony – London 2012 Olympic Games', YouTube, <https://www.youtube. com/watch?v=4As0e4de-rl>

[4] Urwin, W., 'Boer War Memorial', Flickr, < https://www.flickr.com/photos/mals-pics/6501138409/>

References

Altheide, D.L. (2006) *Terrorism and the Politics of Fear*, Lanham, MD: AltaMira Press.

Bleiker, R. (2001) 'The Aesthetic Turn in International Political Theory', *Millennium: Journal of International Studies*, 30(3): 509-533.

Boulton, A. (2008) 'The Popular Geopolitical Wor(l)ds of Post-9/11 Country Music', *Popular Music and Society*, 31(3): 373-387.

Cusick, S.G. (2006) 'Music as Torture/Music as Weapon', *Trans Revista Transcultural De Musica*. Trans10, <http://www.sibetrans.com/trans/article/152/music-as-torture-music-as-weapon>.

Davies, M., Grayson, K. and Philpott, S. (2009) 'Pop Goes IR? Researching the Popular Culture–World Politics Continuum', *Politics*, 29(3): 155-163.

Drezner, D.W. (2009) 'Theory of International Politics and Zombies', *Foreign Policy*, 18 August, <http://foreignpolicy.com/2009/08/18/theory-of-international-politics-and-zombies/>.

Earnest, D.C. and Fish, J.N. (2014) 'Visual Sociology in the Classroom: Using Imagery to Teach the Politics of Globalization', *Politics*, 34(3): 248-262.

Grayson, K. (2014a) 'Drones and Video Games', *E-International Relations*, <http://www.e-ir.info/2014/02/25/drones-and-video-games/>.

Grayson, K. (2014b) 'Metaphorically Speaking, "Where is the Politics?": China, Japan, and the Voldemort Controversy', *E-International Relations*, <http://www.e-ir.info/2014/01/13/metaphorically-speaking-where-is-the-politics-china-japan-and-the-voldemort-controversy/>.

Hannah, E. and Wilkinson, R. (2014) 'Zombies and IR: A Critical Reading', *Politics*, online, <http://onlinelibrary.wiley.com/doi/10.1111/1467-9256.12077/abstract>.

Holland, J. (2014) 'Video Use and the Student Learning Experience in Politics and International Relations', *Politics*, 34(3): 263-274.

Lisle, D. and Pepper, A. (2005) 'The New Face of Global Hollywood: Black Hawk Down and the Politics of Meta-Sovereignty', *Cultural Politics: An International Journal*, 1(2): 165-192.

Mathijs, E. (2006) *Lord of the Rings: Popular Culture in Global Context*, London: Wallflower.

McLaughlin, T. (1998) 'Theory Outside the Academy: Street Smarts and Critical Theory', *Consumption Markets & Culture*, 2(2): 203.

Protevi, J. (2010) 'Rhythm and Cadence, Frenzy and March: Music and the Geo-Bio-Techno-Affective Assemblages of Ancient Warfare', *Theory and Event*, 13(3): 189-211.

Robinson, N. (2015) 'Have You Won the War on Terror? Military Videogames and the State of American Exceptionalism', *Millennium: Journal of International Studies*, 43(2): 450-470.

Rosalndo, R. (1989) 'Imperial Nostalgia', *Representations*, 26(2): 107-122.

Ruane, A.E. and James, P. (2008) 'The International Relations of Middle-Earth: Learning from *The Lord of the Rings*', *International Studies Perspectives*, 9(4): 377-394.

Salter, M.B. (ed.) (2015) *Making Things International 1: Circuits and Motion*, Minneapolis: Minnesota University Press.

Shapiro, M.J. (2010) *The Time of the City: Politics, Philosophy and Genre*, New York, Abingdon, UK: Routledge.

Vitalis, R. (2000) 'The Graceful and Generous Liberal Gesture: Making Racism Invisible in American International Relations', *Millennium: Journal of International Studies*, 29(2): 331-356.

Warde, A. (2005) 'Consumption and Theories of Practice', *Journal of Consumer Culture*, 5(2): 131-153.

Weber, C. (2014) *International Relations Theory: A Critical Introduction* (4th ed.), NewYork: Routledge.

Weldes, J. (2003) *To Seek Out New Worlds: Science Fiction and World Politics*, Basingstoke: Palgrave Macmillan.

Pedagogy and Pop Culture: Pop Culture as Teaching Tool and Assessment Practice

WILLIAM CLAPTON
UNSW AUSTRALIA

Popular culture is today an intrinsic element of social and political life in many societies, particularly those that have reached advanced stages of industrialisation and development. Wherever we go and whatever we do, we are exposed in one way or another to elements of popular culture. The development and advancement of communication networks and technologies, particularly the internet, has only hastened the spread and penetration of popular culture into our everyday lived experiences. As Webber (2005, p. 389) notes, we live in a world of fantasy, exposed to a massive array of both interactive (video games) and passive (movies, TV) fictional entertainment. This is not a particularly novel claim and has been recognised many times before elsewhere, both within and outside the discipline of IR (for example, see Grayson, Davies and Philpott 2009; Ruane and James 2012). The discipline of International Relations (IR) has been generally lethargic, however, in recognising the value of popular culture for both learning and teaching and the production of knowledge about the international.

Still, today there is a growing literature that interrogates the intersections of popular culture and global politics (for example, Der Derian and Shapiro 1989; Weldes 2006; Neumann and Nexon 2006; Carver 2010), and the work of scholars such as Ruane and James (2012, p. 8) has made a strong case for employing popular culture in the classroom. As they and others (Tierney 2007; Dougherty 2002) have argued, using popular culture as a teaching tool can aid in stimulating students and developing their excitement about both the IR courses that they take and the content that is delivered within them. It can also help teachers to ground content (such as relevant IR issues, theories, concepts and events) in a way that is potentially more relatable and accessible to students.

I have used popular culture in my own pedagogical practice in two ways: as a teaching tool for developing understanding, and in assessment practices or regimes. An important caveat here is that what follows is based largely on my own personal observations and experiences and on anecdotal evidence from students and other teaching staff in the courses I have delivered that have actively employed popular culture in learning and teaching. Overall, my general observation is that popular culture can be very effective as a teaching tool when it is used to promote and enhance understanding of complex theories and concepts. It can also be very effective when used as part of a specific assessment or assessment regime. However, popular culture in the learning environment is not without its drawbacks, which I will discuss further below.

I have used popular culture as a teaching tool for the last three years. The initial impetus for doing so was my desire to try to make lectures more interactive and promote active student learning and participation, rather than have students passively sitting and listening (or not listening) to what I was saying. I was also looking for a way to try to make the content more engaging – even I found some of the content delivered in my courses to be overly dry, and one of the areas that I identified for improvement was making my lectures more stimulating and engaging, to encourage students to participate more interactively in my lectures and, to a lesser extent, tutorials.

I resolved in 2012 to begin using popular culture in my lectures as a way of generating greater student interest and engagement. This was consistent both with my own love of all things popular culture and my burgeoning research interest in the area of popular culture and global politics. I took the position (and still do) that the value of popular culture as a vehicle for the construction of knowledge and the development of understanding within the learning environment is significant and, I would argue, fairly obvious. Students today are often completely immersed within various forms of popular culture from a very young age. From movies to television shows to video games, students often come to the IR classroom already steeped and well-versed in popular culture, much more so than the disciplinary knowledge that we seek to impart on them. This is to say that students' understandings of global politics are often shaped in significant ways through their interactions with popular culture for a long period of time before they even arrive in the IR classroom.

It seemed to make sense to me, then, to explore the use of popular culture as a teaching tool, a vehicle through which teachers can explain and develop student understanding of key theories and concepts. Leveraging some of the material that I was reading and writing as I commenced my research in this area in my teaching also seemed like a logical and efficient thing to do. Initially this began as small examples and questions put to students within specific lectures or tutorials – what can we learn about power, political violence and authority, for example, from *Game of Thrones*? Does the zombie genre in general, and specific shows like *The Walking Dead*, offer a useful way of highlighting and understanding competing theoretical perspectives on anarchy and its consequences? In particular, what does it tell us about the specific assumptions regarding humanity's innate nature that inform the perspectives of classical realism and liberalism?

Over the last two academic years (2013 and 2014), this has expanded to include dedicated lectures covering critical IR theories and 'alternative sites of analysis' (popular culture) in both a first-year introductory IR course, and a second-year 'theories and concepts' course. My use, then, of popular culture as a teaching tool has been twofold: first, I have used it to generate greater interest in some of the content I have delivered and promote greater student comprehension and understanding of key IR theories and concepts. Second, I have also invited students to reflect more broadly (and critically) on general methodological and epistemological issues in the discipline, such as what counts as valid forms of knowledge, what the appropriate or legitimate methods are for attaining it, and where we can find them.

I have found students' reaction to the use of popular culture as a way of generating understanding to be broadly positive, and from my own perspective it has seemed, at least anecdotally, to generate greater enthusiasm and interest in both the large (lecture) and small (tutorial) learning environments. Online feedback received after the 2013 iteration of my first-year introductory course, for example, included: 'References to pop culture throughout the course kept it interesting and engaging', and that it was good to be able 'to discuss the content and [be] able to understand international theory through everyday examples like [G]ame of [T]hrones'. Other students commented to me in person after lectures or tutorials that they enjoyed the popular culture examples that were used and found that they made classes more engaging and made it easier to develop their comprehension and understanding of the content that was being delivered. In general, my own experience and the feedback that I received suggested that utilising popular culture artefacts in the learning environment is a useful way of conveying and explaining content that students may sometimes view as arcane or difficult to comprehend.

One interesting observation, however, is that while the majority of students I spoke to or who provided feedback on course evaluation forms appreciated the use of pop culture examples as a way of explaining or describing concepts and theories, reaction was more mixed to the lectures I commenced in 2013 about popular culture as an alternative site of analysis. Several students were rather sceptical about the value of popular culture as a site for conducting analysis and research in the discipline. While they accepted that popular culture was an interesting and engaging way of learning about IR, they were far more reluctant to accept that popular culture could be used to generate and construct knowledge about the international. These students generally seemed to me to fall into one of two groups. The first were those students who rejected the idea of constructing knowledge about the international through the research and analysis of popular culture based on a broader scepticism or rejection of the basic elements of a post-positivist epistemology – namely, the idea of the socially constructed, subjective and inherently partial nature of knowledge.

The second were those students who rejected the idea of popular culture as a site of analysis within the discipline based on their perception that popular culture is just a bit of 'silly fun' and is not really 'serious IR'. This actually feeds into one of the main drawbacks I have experienced thus far in using popular culture as a teaching tool, namely that some students do not take it seriously, or at least do not take it as seriously as they should. That is, using popular culture to try to teach more complex and potentially dry concepts or theories actually seemed to further disengage some students. Related to this, there was another problematic issue I have experienced. When using popular culture as a way of developing understanding of something else, the popular culture example or artefact can overshadow the 'something else' that you are actually trying to teach. In other words, students do not actually apply popular culture to whatever it is that you want them to learn or appropriately engage with, but instead focus only on the popular culture artefact itself.

In one of my tutorials in 2013, I particularly remember telling five students during group discussions on *Game of Thrones* and political violence that the purpose of the discussion was not just to discuss *Game of Thrones* itself (which is what they were doing), but to apply their knowledge and understanding of the show to the issue of political authority and how it manifests internationally. While the students who declined to take popular culture seriously, either as a learning tool or as a site of research and analysis, were a minority, it is still an issue that I am grappling with: how do I encourage students to engage seriously when I employ popular culture? How do I encourage them to see beyond the sheer novelty and entertainment value of using popular culture sources in the learning environment and connect with the actual content that I am attempting to deliver? This is not to suggest that popular culture is not useful or that this drawback is insurmountable, but it is something that teachers need to be aware of when employing pop culture in their teaching and learning practice.

I also set two formative learning activities (therefore no marks available) in a second-year undergraduate course on IR theories and concepts. The first tasked students with conducting a short analysis (approximately 500 words) of what one of two artefacts tell us about international law and order: the film *Team America: World Police* and a video of a panel on 'The War on Whistleblowers' held as part of the Sydney Opera House's 'Ideas at the House' panel series. The second activity tasked students with preparing a 500-word analysis of a meme of their choosing that related to one or more of the course topics and themes. One of the key lessons I wanted students to take away from the exercises was that there are critical possibilities evident in sites of analysis beyond the IR textbook, article or monograph, the things that are published by experts. Critically reflecting on and engaging with theories issues or concepts associated with the international need not only take place within the specific sites or forums that we in the academy have constructed. While I am certainly not arguing that conventional disciplinary 'outputs' are not useful and important in terms of both teaching and research, the idea that these outputs are the only legitimate or valid arenas through which knowledge about international relations can be produced feeds into the general disciplinary narrative that only IR experts and practitioners (states-persons, diplomats, etc.) are 'doing' IR.

What I wanted students to see and appreciate is that IR is 'done' in many forums and in many ways that are sometimes far removed from the worlds of scholars and practitioners, that 'normal' people do IR on a daily basis. Ultimately, I wanted my students to begin to reposition themselves as something other than passive learners of what experts tell them IR is. More specifically, I wanted (and continue to want) my students to see themselves as active learners and 'doers' of IR, to recognise that they are actively involved in the production of knowledge and understanding, and to engage with other 'everyday' people who are doing IR in areas and sites with which my students are potentially more familiar – memes, the internet, film, TV, etc.

In terms of the impact and efficacy of the activities, I will say first that they both proved to be very popular with my students, particularly the memes analysis activity, which was embraced by students to such an extent that some of them not only analysed memes, but created memes of me (with rather humorous and incisive comments based on things I had said or done during the lectures). The analyses provided in both exercises were also of a generally very good quality, with a number of excellent, standout analyses provided. In the second activity, in which students were required to analyse memes, for example, the range of memes and topics covered was diverse, ranging from the ways in which critical perspectives are devalued in mainstream disciplinary discourse to the way in which gendered norms of heterosexuality serve to reproduce both gendered understandings of 'male' and 'female' and ultimately political actors and depoliticised subjects. Ultimately, though, the most pleasing aspect of the activity was that several students appeared to grasp and acknowledge that politics takes place at sites beyond the IR text. Several students conveyed to me not only the fun that they had in completing the activities, but also their interest and enthusiasm at being able to engage substantively with the politics of selected popular culture artefacts.

It should be noted, however, that these formative assessments had a very specific purpose, to impress upon students that there are potentially valuable insights to be gleaned from popular culture, one that went beyond simply developing and testing students' understandings of specific content. That is, popular culture and its appropriateness as a site of analysis in IR were a substantive component of what I wanted students to learn, understand and appreciate as part of completing these activities. Popular culture was not simply a vehicle for learning about something else. This is potentially beyond how others might use or employ popular culture as part of their assessment practices and of course may not be fit for other courses, depending on the teacher's own particular purposes. The activities were also formative and did not contribute to student's overall grades for the course. At face value, I did (and continue to) question whether this encouraged students to be more 'adventurous' and creative in the analyses that they produced for both activities. While I have no significant or substantive evidence to prove or disprove this, I do wonder whether students might have approached the activities differently had marks been allocated to them.

In conclusion, popular culture has much to offer as a teaching and learning tool. My experiences have been generally positive and I intend to continue to explore ways in which I can integrate popular culture into my teaching practice, both in terms of delivering content in the classroom and as part of the assessments that I set in my courses. While popular culture is not without its potential problems and pitfalls, it offers differing, potentially more accessible insights about the international that generally are not found in standard IR textbooks. This is not to say that traditional methods of learning and teaching in IR or traditional disciplinary artefacts are not as valuable or are not valuable in general, far from it. However, it is to contend, based on my experiences, that our students and we potentially have much to gain in terms of the quality of our teaching, the student experience in the learning environment, and ultimately students' realisation of the learning outcomes that we set in our courses, from diversifying and broadening our teaching practices to include popular culture.

References

Carver, T. (2010) 'Cinematic Ontologies and Viewer Epistemologies: Knowing International Politics as Moving Images', *Global Society*, 24(3): 421-31.

Der Derian, J. and M. Shapiro, (eds)(1989) *International/Intertextual Relations: Postmodern Readings of World Politics*, Lanham, MD: Lexington.

Dougherty, B.K. (2002) 'Comic Relief: Using Political Cartoons in the Classroom', *International Studies Perspectives*, 3(3): 258-70.

Grayson, K., M. Davies and S. Philpott (2009) 'Pop Goes IR? Researching the Popular Culture – World Politics Continuum', *Politics*, 29(3): 155-63.

Nexon, D.H. and I.B. Neumann (eds) (2006) *Harry Potter and International Relations*, Lanham, MD: Rowman & Littlefield.

Ruane, A.E. and P. James (2012) *The International Relations of Middle Earth: Learning From The Lord of the Rings*, Ann Arbor: University of Michigan.

Tierney, M.J. (2007) 'Schoolhouse Rock: Pedagogy, Politics, and Pop', *International Studies Perspectives*, 8(1): iii-v.

Webber, J. (2005) 'Independence Day as a Cosmopolitan Moment: Teaching International Relations', *International Studies Perspectives*, 2(3): 281-87.

Weldes, J. (2006) 'High Politics and Low Data: Globalization Discourses and Popular Culture', in D. Yanow and P. Schwartz-Shea (eds) *Interpretation and Method: Empirical Research Methods and the Interpretive Turn*, New York: M.E. Sharpe, 176-86.

Contributors

Linda Åhäll is a Lecturer in International Relations at Keele University, UK, and also currently Postdoctoral Researcher in the Militarization 2.0 project at Malmö University, Sweden. Her research explores the crossroads of gender politics and security studies, often through popular culture, and contributes to feminist security studies as well as studies of visual global politics and the politics of emotions. She has published in journals such as *Security Dialogue*, the *International Feminist Journal of Politics* and *Critical Studies on Security;* is the co-editor of *Gender, Agency and Political Violence* (2002) and *Emotions, Politics and War* (2015); and is very happy that her monograph *Sexing War/Policing Gender: Motherhood, Myth and Women's Political Violence* was published as part of Routledge's book series, Popular Culture and World Politics, in March 2015.

Roland Bleiker is a Professor of International Relations at the University of Queensland. His current research examines how images, and the emotions they engender, shape responses to humanitarian crises. Recent publications include *Aesthetics and World Politics* (Palgrave, 2009/2012) and, as co-editor, a forum on 'Emotions and World Politics' in *International Theory* (volume 3, 2014).

Daniel Bos is a PhD candidate based in the Geography Department at Newcastle University, UK. His research interests focus on the intersections between the military, world politics and popular culture. His current research examines the popular geopolitics of military-themed video games. This has involved detailed analysis of the geopolitical and militaristic content of video games, their production, and players' interactions and understandings.

William Clapton is a Lecturer in International Relations at UNSW Australia. His research interests include risk and hierarchy in international relations; the foreign and defence policies of Australia, India and the United States; and the intersections between popular culture and world politics. He is the author of *Risk and Hierarchy in International Society: Liberal Interventionism in the Post-Cold War Era*, recently published with Palgrave Macmillan, and has published on risk and hierarchy in *International Politics* and *International Relations*.

Matt Davies is a Senior Lecturer in International Political Economy at Newcastle University, UK. He is a co-editor for the Routledge book series, Popular Culture and World Politics, as well as the degree programme director for Newcastle's Master of Arts in World Politics and Popular Culture. In addition to writing about punk rock, he has written on Buffy the Vampire Slayer (in *International Political Sociology*, 2010) and on video clips about the financial crisis (in *Alternatives*, 2012).

Jason Dittmer is a Reader in Human Geography at University College London and author of *Popular Culture, Geopolitics, and Identity* (Rowman and Littlefield, 2010) and *Captain America and the Nationalist Superhero: Metaphors, narratives, and geopolitics* (Temple University Press, 2013). His current research is on diplomacy and assemblage.

Klaus Dodds is a Professor of Geopolitics at Royal Holloway, University of London, and author of many books, including *Geopolitics: A Very Short Introduction* (OUP 2014) and *International Politics and Film* (Columbia University Press 2014 with Sean Carter).

Constance Duncombe is a Postdoctoral Research Fellow in the School of Political Science and International Studies at the University of Queensland. Her current research examines how representations trigger emotions that drive the struggle for recognition, with a particular focus on the Iran-US relationship. Her work has appeared in *Global Change, Peace and Security* (2011), *Global Discourse* (2014), and in the edited volume *The Contemporary Middle East: Revolution or Reform?* (2014).

Marianne Franklin is a Professor of Global Media and Politics at Goldsmiths, University of London. Her latest book, *Digital Dilemmas: Power, Resistance and the Internet*, is out with Oxford University Press. She is working on her next book, a study of the cultural geopolitics of musical sampling. Her Twitter handle is @GloComm.

Kyle Grayson is a Senior Lecturer in International Politics at Newcastle University, UK. He is a lead editor of the journal *Politics*, an associate editor of *Critical Studies* on Security and a co-editor of the *Popular Culture and World Politics* book series.

Nicholas Kiersey is an Associate Professor in Political Science at Ohio University. Recent works of his have been published in the *Journal of Critical Globalization Studies*, *Global Society* and *Global Discourse*. He recently co-edited the volume *Battlestar Galactica and International Relations* with Iver Neumann (Routledge, 2013). His current book project is entitled *Negotiating Crisis: Neoliberal Power in Austerity Ireland*, and is set to be published by Rowman & Littlefield in 2015.

Iver B. Neumann is Montague Burton Professor of International Relations at the London School of Economics. He co-edited *Harry Potter and International Relations* with Dan Nexon and *Battlestar Galactica and International Relations* with Nick Kiersey.

Nick Robinson is an Associate Professor in Politics/Videogames research at the University of Leeds. He has published widely in journals such as *Millennium: Journal of International Studies*, *Political Studies*, *JCMS: Journal of Common Market Studies*, the *Political Quarterly* and the *Journal of Power*. He is author of a couple of books and is presently working on a book for the Popular Culture and World Politics book series (Routledge) entitled *Videogames, Popular Culture and World Politics*. He is also presently working as part of an international research team on a four-year Framework Grant from the Swedish Research Council as part of its programme, 'The Digitized Society: Past, Present, and Future'. Their project, 'Militarization 2.0: Militarization's Social Media Footprint Through a Gendered Lens', involves project partners from Sweden, the UK and Germany.

Christina Rowley is a Research Associate in the School of Sociology, Politics and International Studies at the University of Bristol, UK. She studies the various intersections between popular culture and world politics, often with a particular focus on gender and/or US foreign policy. Her work has appeared in *Security Dialogue*, the *British Journal of Politics and International Relations* and the *International Feminist Journal of Politics*. Her current research focuses on the ways in which mainstream IR, as a set of disciplinary practices, both incorporates and marginalises popular culture as a legitimate object of study.

Saara Särmä is a feminist, an artist and a researcher in International Relations at the University of Tampere, Finland, where she received a doctorate in 2014. Saara's doctoral dissertation, *Junk Feminism and Nuclear Wannabe: Collaging Parodies of Iran and North Korea*, focused on internet parody images and memes, and developed a unique art-based collage methodology for studying world politics. She's interested in politics of visuality, feminist academic activism, and laughter in world politics. Currently she is working on developing the visual collage methodology further as both a research and a pedagogical tool and is experimenting with collective possibilities of collaging. Her artwork can be seen at www.huippumisukka.fi.

Robert A. Saunders is a Professor in the Department of History and Political Science at Farmingdale State College, SUNY. The author of three books, including *The Many Faces of Sacha Baron Cohen: Politics, Parody, and the Battle over Borat* (2008), his research explores the impact of popular culture on geopolitics, nationalism and religious identity. His research has appeared in *Progress in Human Geography*, the *Slavic Review*, *Nations and Nationalism*, *Geopolitics* and other journals. He also is the curator of the 'Popular Culture and IR' blog channel at E-International Relations.

Michael J. Shapiro is a Professor of Political Science at the University of Hawaii, Manoa. His most recent book is *War Crimes, Atrocity, and Justice* (Polity, 2015).

Jutta Weldes is a Professor of International Relations at the University of Bristol, UK. Her current research interests centre on, among other things, popular culture and world politics. In this area, she has written on *Star Trek* and US foreign policy, Issac Asimov's SF and globalisation, the Buffyverse, and the theorisation of in/security (with Christina Rowley), and is editor of *To Seek Out New Worlds: Science Fiction and World Politics* (Palgrave: 2003). She is also the author of *Constructing National Interests: The United States and the Cuban Missile Crisis* (University of Minnesota Press, 1999), co-editor of *Cultures of Insecurity: States, Communities, and the Production of Danger* (University of Minnesota Press, 1999), and has published in such journals as *International Studies Quarterly*, *Security Dialogue*, the *European Journal of International Relations*, *Millennium* and the *British Journal of Politics and International Relations*.